ARCHAEOLOGY
IS RUBBISH

A Beginner's Guide

ARCHAEOLOGY IS RUBBISH

A Beginner's Guide

TONY ROBINSON

and

PROFESSOR MICK ASTON

First published 2002 by Channel 4 Books
This edition published 2003 by Channel 4 Books
an imprint of Pan Macmillan Ltd
Pan Macmillan, 20 New Wharf Road, London N1 9RR
Basingstoke and Oxford

Associated companies throughout the world

www.panmacmillan.com

ISBN 0 7522 1530 2

Design by designsection, Frome, Somerset
Illustrations by Oxford Designers and Illustrators
Colour reproduction by Aylesbury Studios
Printed and bound in Great Britain by Butler & Tanner Limited, Frome and London

Acknowledgements

T his book is for Phil Harding, a good man, a great friend, and a superb archaeologist. It's also dedicated to the army of highly qualified, underpaid diggers whose commitment to high standards helps make British archaeological techniques among the best in the world.

Many thanks for their help to Professor Margaret Cox, Bob Croft, Kerry Ely, Dr Helen Geake, Dr Chris Gaffney, Phil Harding, Andrew Jackson and David Neal, and to Guy de la Bédoyère for steering us through the thorny issues raised by Chapter 13. Any insightful observations are theirs. Any mistakes are ours.

As always, we're deeply indebted to Teresa Hall and Heledd Mathias for help, support and encouragement, and also for typing and proof-reading.

Finally, a big thank you to Professor Philip Rahtz, whose teaching, archaeology and example have been a profound inspiration to us.

Lara Croft smashes her way into an ancient pyramid jam-packed with skeletons, glittering treasure and mechanical booby-traps. She grabs a creeper and swings effortlessly across a cobra-ridden underground vault, snatches a golden goblet from a crumbling stone altar and then, fending off spiders the size of dinner plates, she retreats into the dense jungle while the entire edifice collapses around her.

This is how archaeology is portrayed worldwide by Hollywood and the computer games industry. But such glossy images of theft and destruction bear little relation to the windswept fields full of apparently featureless gravel where real-life British archaeologists eke out a living. No golden goblets for them. If they're lucky they'll find a few smashed pots, a snapped brooch, a bent dagger-handle or a piece of burnt doorframe.

Yes, archaeology isn't glamour, it's rubbish! Once upon a time this bashed and broken material was thrown away by our forebears. The raw material with which archaeologists work is the waste discarded by an infinitely long line of Stone Age tool-makers, Roman housewives, Norman potters, Tudor carpenters, Stuart pipe-makers and Victorian factory workers. British archaeology is the history of our nation's waste disposal.

But why was it never cleared away? Why is so much of Britain metres thick in the decayed waste dropped by thousands of years of litterbugs? One of the biggest problems in our ancestors' lives was how to dispose of the things they didn't want. Before 1900 there was no such thing as a council rubbish collection. Getting rid of your waste was your problem and yours alone. Recycling wasn't an optional extra for the well-meaning middle classes. Everybody did it. If your waste was edible you gave it to your pigs. If it was metal you melted it down. But what about the bulk of totally useless everyday stuff? Country-dwellers chucked it on their dung-heap, and later it was spread on the fields mixed up with the horse-manure and cow-dung. Townfolk dug a big hole and buried it in their garden, and when that hole was full they dug another one. That's why nowadays you can walk across virtually any field in Britain and you'll find a host of glass fragments, pottery sherds and broken clay pipes.

And if you excavate an old town you'll find layer upon layer of dark soil stuffed with ancient bits and pieces – evidence of centuries of dumped urban rubbish.

And it wasn't just domestic waste that was a problem. There was the human kind too. The earliest mains drainage is only 150 years old. Before that most people did their business in a hole in the ground, and when they'd filled it they got out their spade and looked for another suitable site. These ancient cesspits now provide archaeologists with a rich haul of lost finds. When Auntie dropped her porridge spoon down the privy she wasn't likely to roll her sleeve up and attempt to get it back. However valuable it might have been, there are some lucky dips that just aren't worth taking part in.

Human waste was often transported too. Early each morning carts would arrive in every British town laden with fruit and vegetables, and would leave a few hours later brimful of so-called 'night soil'. Auntie's porridge spoon might well end up deposited on a field five miles away along with the rest of the manure.

But if archaeology is rubbish, why bother to dig it up, write books about it, and spend a fortune preserving it?

At first glance it's certainly a bizarre ritual. The smashed piss-pot that a Tudor farmer carelessly lobbed on his dung-heap is now meticulously excavated over several days, the pieces washed, labelled, catalogued, photographed and drawn for an academic report, before being taken to a laboratory for conservation and restoration, and finally put on display in a glass case. Or, an even worse fate, they're stored unseen for a hundred years in a cardboard box in a specially controlled environment in a museum, only to be opened in the unlikely event that some sad archaeology student will want to write his thesis on rural Tudor bedroom pottery

It's a little difficult to understand why anyone in their right mind would want to go through this long process of excavation, restoration and storage, let alone fund it. But in fact this cornucopia of junk tells us far more about what was going on in the past than a thousand golden goblets seized from a thousand spider-infested temple altars.

Of course it's exciting to pluck some jewel-encrusted piece of treasure out of the earth, but such finds are unlikely to help us understand much about the person who wore them or made them. And the interminable problems that a valuable find will throw up are a distinct disincentive. How do you to find out who legally owns it?

Do you really want to end up in a coroner's court or caught up in some complicated legal wrangle? Who's going to insure it? Who's going to conserve it and how much will the premium be? Who's going to look after it and where can it be securely stored? Most real Indiana Joneses would much rather discover an ancient Canaanite peasant's hovel than the Ark of the Covenant – it would be just as interesting and much less of a hassle.

So if you're only interested in archaeology because you think it's an exciting way to get your hands on a few irreplaceable and consequently valuable artefacts, close this book right now and hire the video of *Raiders of the Lost Ark* instead. But if you fancy trawling through a mire of ancient rubbish in order to bring back to life the story of your ancestors, pull on your overcoat, woolly hat and wellingtons, get out into your back garden and dig a hole.

CHAPTER 1

But don't start digging straight away. The first thing to do is look. If you explore the back garden of any house in any town anywhere in Britain, you're likely to come across a wealth of archaeological rubbish in the topsoil.

What have you got in your garden? There are bits of coal and charcoal. Ash from old fires and burnt garden rubbish. You can see little bits of white glazed ceramic, remnants of cups, plates, saucers and gravy dishes. It may not look much. It may have been in use until pretty recently. You probably see it every time you dig the flowerbeds and you usually ignore it. But it's the top layer of your garden's archaeology.

Look under the rose bushes. There's a bit of blue and white pottery. Is it from Woolworth's? Could it be from a nineteenth-century table-service? It might just be sixteenth- or seventeenth-century Delft-ware imported from Holland. Rarer still, it could be Chinese bone china or porcelain, the inspiration behind countless later mass-produced willow-pattern tea-sets. Put it in a box and make a note that you found it on the surface of your garden. Later you'll need to label it properly.

Everywhere there are pieces of red-fired clay. Some of them are smashed bits of flowerpot, but you also find lumps of brick, the debris from demolished buildings. Before Mr Marley invented his roof tile and Mr Breeze invented his block, there were 200 years in which brick was the bog-standard building material all over the country.

There are dozens of bits of purply-blue slate, miles away from their original source. In the eighteenth century, once Britain's canal networks were in place, the whole country had a cheap new standardized roofing material available to it – slates from the quarries of North Wales. If you're really lucky, your fragments may turn out to be from a school writing slate, but you're unlikely to be able to tell unless you find the slate pencil that goes with it. It'll look a bit like a knitting needle. You poke around for a few minutes. You find a walnut shell, but no slate pencil.

Then things start to get more interesting. You turn up some thicker, much rougher pieces of pottery. One is orangey-red, the others are brownish-yellow and they're glazed on the inside but not on the outside. This is to make them cheap to produce. The insides were glazed so they'd hold water, but the outsides didn't need to be watertight so were left untouched. They're products of old country potteries. People didn't buy this stuff from a shop – it was transported from village to village in a cart. These fragments are the last remaining evidence of a rural industry that produced the nation's pots for centuries, before they were superseded by cheaper, mass-produced goods from the pot-banks of Stoke-on-Trent.

You find bits of stoneware too, grey on the inside and shiny on the outside. There's even a little piece with letters stamped on it. It's a fragment of a storage jar, a forerunner of the large plastic containers we use for storing antifreeze or cheap wine.

And of course your garden's riddled with glass. The flat thin pieces are from windows, the curved bits are bottle glass. The clear stuff is likely to be from the nineteenth or twentieth century. But you've also got a few little pieces that look pretty exotic, as multicoloured as a peacock's feather. They're probably from the seventeenth or eighteenth century and the vivid colouring is caused by corrosive elements in the soil. Whether or not the glass is transparent depends on changes that have occurred in the glass-making process through the ages. As a rule of thumb, Roman glass is clear, bits from the medieval period to the eighteenth century are coloured by the soil, and modern glass is transparent again.

Up to the sixteenth century, glass was so valuable that if you moved house you took your windows with you. Bottles became standard containers only in the late eighteenth century, but even then they were quite valuable. If you were

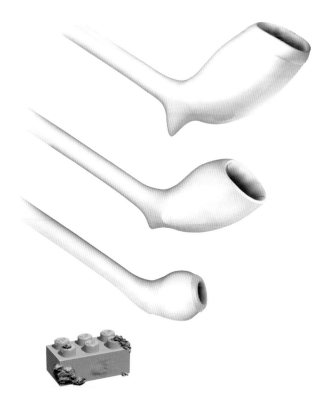

wealthy enough, you'd buy a barrel of wine and decant it into bottles. But you didn't get rid of the empties – you washed them and refilled them. And in case your guests were tempted to take them home under their coats, you put your own stamp on the neck of each bottle. Gradually though, more and more bottles were mass produced and beer bottles, milk bottles and wine bottles became cheap enough to discard.

You discover two little round things that look like plain glass marbles. In fact they're trophies retrieved by schoolboys a hundred or so years ago. Long before the invention of the aluminium can, children used to smash fizzy drink bottles in order to get at the glass ball that sealed in the gas.

You pick up a handful of little clay rods that look a bit like the white plastic tubes that are wrapped round present-day electrical wiring. You've no idea what they are. When you look more closely you can see that some of them have black stains on them. Then you find a tell-tale matching bowl and realize they're the broken stems of clay pipes, blackened by the act of smoking. These are the fag ends of history. Sir Walter Raleigh introduced us to nicotine in Tudor times, but it wasn't until the seventeenth century that pipe-smoking caught on in a big way. By the 1800s the upper classes had rejected the pipe in favour of the cigar, and it was the poor who were now toking away on clay pipes. But fired clay is brittle and the pipes kept snapping. They usually started out their life about half a metre long (the so-called churchwarden's pipe), but every time one snapped, its owner discarded the broken piece and the bowl got that bit closer to his nose, until finally it broke or his nose hairs got so singed he threw the stubby end away.

The style of the bowls changed over time. The original ones were small and barrel-shaped, and only big enough to hold a pea-sized piece of tobacco. Later they became larger and sat upright on the pipe stem. Many had stamps on them advertising the maker or place of manufacture, so often pieces of pipe, particularly the bowls, can be identified to within a decade of a particular pipe-maker's career. This can be extremely useful dating evidence.

Apart from all this debris, you hit on other little treasures – a plastic soldier out of an old cereal packet, the chassis from a Dinky car, a Lego brick. There's a little brown ball that looks a bit like the glass bottle marbles, but is actually a real old marble made of fired clay. There are metal bits and pieces – nails, hairpins, buckles from belts and bags and horse harnesses, fragments from tin labels and boxes, as well as buttons and screws. There are also little pieces from a long-discarded, ceramic figure – a stray arm, a severed head, and an unattributable piece of torso.

All this junk is archaeology. It tells us how people lived over the last two or three hundred years, the richest period for archaeology our planet has yet known. From the seventeenth century onwards there was an explosion in the number of ordinary bits and pieces made for ordinary human beings. For instance, the buttons you found became common only in the eighteenth century, and screws were invented only a hundred or so years ago. Not only were there more people, but they could afford more things, most of which were made out of tough, newly available materials that didn't decay or rot, and so are still there for you, the intrepid archaeologist, to rediscover in your back garden.

So many finds, so much history, and you haven't even broken sweat yet.

CHAPTER 2

So how did archaeology begin? From the moment the first pyramid was built, people hung around outside it and tried to dig their way in. As soon as the volcano at Pompeii started to cool, there were folk hacking away at the petrified town attempting to get their hands on the discarded booty.

Treasure-hunting has always played an important part in the development of archaeology, and so has recycling. Wall-robbing has probably been going on since the collapse of the very first stone house on the planet. On summer days in the twelfth century the monks of St Albans would climb to the top of their church tower. Below they could see the dried grass lines that showed them where the foundations of the Roman city of Verulamium still lay below the surface of

I've been taking photographs of old buildings and archaeology all my life. This is the Norman central tower of the abbey church at St Albans. It was from here that the monks looked out over the site of the Roman city of Verulamium in order to spot potential building materials. The tower itself is built of recycled Roman bricks – Mick.

These impressive ruins are all that remain of the medieval monastic church at Much Wenlock, Shropshire. This is where monks dug up the reputed remains of St Milburga in the twelfth century.

their fields. They hadn't made the climb for the exercise or out of academic interest. They wanted cheap building materials with low transport costs. But who's to say that when they dug for free recyclable bricks and stone, they weren't also fascinated by what they uncovered?

That was certainly the case at Much Wenlock in Shropshire. In AD 1101 the old church was falling to pieces and two boys fell down a hole in the floor and discovered a skeleton. The local monks knew from an old document that their patron saint, St Milburga, was buried by the side of a long-lost altar, so in order to verify that the body was hers they did what countless archaeologists have done ever since – they dug in all directions. Then, once they'd discovered the missing altar, they washed their 'find', the newly authenticated skeleton of St Milburga, before putting it on display in a brand-new shrine. Once again, this wasn't pure academic research, but then how much archaeology actually is?

In 1191, a hundred miles away in Glastonbury, another dig took place. There the monks unearthed two more skeletons. Quite quickly they realized that these were the remains of the renowned King Arthur and Guinevere, his second wife. How did they know? Because a lead cross was found next to the bones and it said: 'Here lies the renowned King Arthur with Guinevere his

The alleged site of the graves of Arthur and Guinevere at Glastonbury Abbey, Somerset.

second wife'. What a lucky break! Particularly because the abbey had burnt down not long before, and these new relics would attract religious tourists and money. The king was pleased too, because having the bodies of two such internationally famous celebrities in his possession gave him a great deal of credibility. All of a sudden the future of Glastonbury Abbey looked rosy. Was this an example of God moving in a mysterious way? No. The inscription was later shown to be a fake. Nevertheless, it placed the monks of Glastonbury Abbey well and truly in the history books as having perpetrated the first recorded example of archaeological fraud.

But were people in the Middle Ages interested in ruins only as a source of building materials and prestige? Didn't it occur to them that their ancient monuments could tell them countless fascinating stories about the lives of their ancestors? Certainly most people, even the uneducated poor, were vaguely aware that the Romans had occupied Britain for the best part of four centuries and had left a massive crumbling heritage behind them. But not much other ancient architecture appears to have been understood – or even noticed. The great historian Bede, writing in the eighth century, attempted to chronicle the whole story of the people of Britain, but didn't even mention Stonehenge. Until the sixteenth century, people who were aware of those massive stones on Salisbury Plain thought they were an African monument that had been manhandled by giants across the Mediterranean and set down in Ireland to be used as the walls for an enormous bath-house. The stones were then supposed to have been magically hijacked by Merlin, who dropped them on Salisbury Plain to commemorate King Arthur's victory over the Saxons.

It was another 350 years before scientists began to realize precisely how old Stonehenge is. But even now we don't really know what it was for. Maybe today's theories will seem to future generations as unlikely as the yarn about the giants' washing facilities.

So if they were ignored for so long, how did people get to learn about our ancient British monuments? The first person we know of who was sufficiently interested in old ruins to describe them in detail was a priest called Gerald who lived in the late twelfth century. He went on a tour round Wales with his bishop to persuade the local people to fight in the crusades, and wrote an account of his journey in which he describes the monuments he saw. He had a really good eye for architecture and noticed things that passed other people by. For instance, this is how he described the ruined fortress at Caerleon: 'Many traces of its former splendour can still be seen. Immense palaces originally ornamented with gilded roofs in imitation of Roman magnificence. You'll find on all sides, both inside and outside the circuit of the walls, underground buildings and passages, aqueducts and what I think worthy of note, stoves constructed with wonderful art to transmit the heat insensibly through narrow tubes passing up the side walls.' In other words, Gerald of Wales had discovered a Roman central heating system!

It's easy to see why antiquarians in the seventeenth century were so excited by Stonehenge, although at that time it was more ruined than it is now. Several stones were re-erected in the twentieth century.

Nowadays it's almost impossible for us to imagine a time when our monuments weren't described and catalogued. But the earliest example we have of someone drawing up a detailed list of old ruins isn't until 1478. William Worcester had spent his working life as secretary to Sir John Fastolf (the inspiration for Shakespeare when he created the lecherous drunk Falstaff in *Henry IV*). On his retirement, once rid of his apparently stingy employer, William took a two-year holiday during which he wandered from Norfolk to Cornwall, describing in detail the churches, ruined castles, town walls, even the huge carved hill figures he came across.

A more eccentric search took place in the 1530s. A young deacon called John Leland was instructed by King Henry VIII to search the country's monastic book stores for important texts and volumes in order that they could be brought 'out of deadly darkness into lively light'. In practice this simply meant that when Henry closed down the monasteries a lot of nice books ended up in his palace. But while Leland was travelling round the countryside he obsessively recorded the various old buildings he came across. This was the first time the existence of many of these places was identified. For nearly 200 years his writings lay on the shelf, ignored as the ramblings of a crank. They were eventually published in 1710 but it wasn't until the early twentieth century that their true value was realized, and they now give us a unique picture of England at the end of the Middle Ages.

John White's painting of native Americans dancing in a wooden circle.

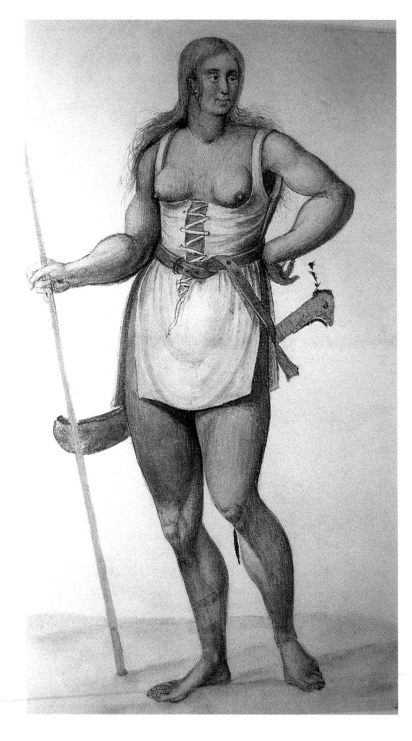

John White's painting of what he imagined an Ancient British woman would have looked like.

Henry's motivation appears to have been plunder, and the whole exercise apparently drove Leland completely and irrevocably mad. But both Leland and William Worcester demonstrate that people were beginning to look at the past through Britain's buildings and its landscape.

This new pseudo-science soon acquired a name. It was called antiquarianism. It really began to take off when the first explorers returned from the Americas. They brought home with them tales of a wild people they called the Indians. Sixteenth-century scholars were enthralled by these painted savages. They seemed to be perfect examples of the kind of people who would have inhabited Britain in the dim and distant past. Tudor artists drew vivid sketches of Indian timber circles that looked rather like Stonehenge, and the dancing natives they created bear a striking resemblance to characters out of Disney's *Pocahontas*. The bare-breasted, blue-painted, sword-wielding women drawn by explorer and draughtsman John White may not be historically accurate, but you can imagine them being scrutinized for many a long evening by the earnest members of the Royal Society.

It was the fact that these primitive people used only stone tools that made the antiquarians really excited. Thousands of large shiny stones had been discovered in Britain in the Middle Ages, but no one realized what they were. They were thought to have been caused by thunderbolts or created by the fairies, and they were traded as magical totems to be hung up in the roof to ward off lightning and stop the house burning down. But now, when they were compared with Indian tools, it became apparent that these strange, beautiful, shiny artefacts were in fact polished stone axes knapped by our most ancient ancestors. The story of our prehistory was starting to emerge.

John Aubrey, diarist and antiquarian (1626-97).

The great antiquarian John Aubrey (1626–97) was the first person to work out that Britain's stone circles were pre-Roman and stemmed from the age when people were using these axes. He captured the imagination of his patron King Charles II after visiting the stones at Avebury, a site which until then seems to have been completely overlooked. 'His Majestie,' writes Aubrey, 'commanded me to digge at the bottom of the stones… to try if I could find any humane bones: but I did not doe it' – although whether this was out of laziness or a praiseworthy desire to preserve Britain's heritage isn't recorded.

But the seventeenth century wasn't just a time for riding round the countryside searching for previously undiscovered sites. It was also the beginning of the great age of collecting. The wealthy began acquiring their own private collections of interesting artefacts. One of the most notorious collectors was Elias Ashmole, a servant of the king, who learnt about a fascinating collection in the possession of the explorer John Tradescant and his wife Hester, and offered to catalogue it. He then bullied the pair into leaving it to him in their will. John later changed his mind and made another will bequeathing his collection to the king, but on John's death Elias swiftly moved in next door to Hester to make sure she didn't give it away or sell any of it off. Nine years later the poor woman was found drowned in her garden pond. On hearing the news, Elias promptly removed all her paintings and acquired the lease of her house and garden.

From these shabby beginnings emerged the first public museum in Britain: the Ashmolean opened in 1683. Although Elias's name is still remembered as its founder, the Tradescants aren't completely forgotten either. While out collecting new botanical specimens in Virginia, they gave their name to the Tradescantia, the small houseplant that now collects dust on British window ledges from Bodmin to Inverness.

The great bank and ditch of the henge monument at Avebury in Wiltshire, with its internal stone circles, was first recorded by Aubrey and Stukeley. Some of the stones were pulled down and buried in the Middle Ages and later re-erected by Alexander Keiller, the marmalade millionaire, in the twentieth century.

*William Stukeley, the surveyor
of Stonehenge (1687-1765).*

By the eighteenth century, educated, middle-class men were measuring and recording the things they saw all over the world, and those observations began to be refined into a series of sciences. This was as true of archaeology as it was of geography, geology and natural history. William Stukeley (1687-1765) a doctor turned vicar, meticulously measured Stonehenge. He also excavated burials there, the first record we have of a real archaeological dig. It led him to believe that the barrows weren't, as had previously been thought, constructed for the dead after some great battle, but were pre-Roman 'sepulchres of kings and great personages buried during a considerable space of time, and that in peace'. Stukeley's fieldwork is remarkably sophisticated for the period but unfortunately, by the time it was published in 1740, he'd radically reviewed his ideas. He was now obsessed by Druids and had come to believe they'd constructed both Avebury and Stonehenge. He even dressed up as a high priest and performed the occasional Druidic rite. In hindsight this may seem a bit daft, but sadly he also altered his findings in order to strengthen his case, and is ultimately responsible for the lasting and entirely false association between Druidism and the great stone rings. To give him his due, he was the first person to state publicly that our stone circles are under threat from plunder and ill use. But it's ironic that his fraudulent science should have been the inspiration that led to the chaos we now see on Salisbury Plain every midsummer solstice.

By the early nineteenth century, digging up old artefacts had become a hobby for educated gentlemen. Their wives and daughters would lay out a picnic and watch while their intrepid menfolk supervised the local estate labourers in the pillage of Britain's ancient long barrows and round barrows. The urns and arrowheads they dug for usually ended up in the nearby Great House where they would take their place in a cabinet of curiosities alongside similar finds from Turkey, Greece and Egypt.

But exactly how old were these trophies? In the seventeenth century Archbishop James Ussher (1581–1656) had worked out from his biblical studies that the world had been created in the year 4004 BC. This date was even printed for information in the margin of the new version of the Bible commissioned by King James I. But nineteenth-century science was casting serious doubt on this calculation. Throughout Europe it was becoming clear to geologists that the processes needed to form layers of rock, fossils and river deposits took far longer than the timeframe allowed by Archbishop Ussher. In addition some very old layers contained man-made tools, so it looked as though human beings had been on the planet for much longer than had been previously realized.

Then in 1859 Charles Darwin published *On the Origin of Species*, and it confirmed that not only had plants and animals evolved over millennia, but that people and their tools had developed over a very long timescale too.

Museum curators possessed sack-loads of old tools, but didn't know how to categorize the periods in which they'd been made. Finally a Dane called Christian Thomsen (who died in 1865) decided to name them by the materials from which

Eighteenth-century gentlemen and labourers digging a barrow while the ladies look on.

Eighteenth-century gentlemen and ladies sheltering in the barrow from inclement weather.

they were made – stone, bronze and iron. The deepest finds were stone, the shallowest iron, so it seemed plain that this was the right chronological order. The Three Age System – Stone Age, Bronze Age and Iron Age – was born.

Then in 1880 one man completely revolutionized archaeology. A sickly ex-army surveyor called Augustus Lane-Fox, who'd collected antiquities all over the world, inherited a large estate on the border between Wiltshire and Dorset on condition that he changed his name to that of its previous owner, Pitt-Rivers. He agreed and set about excavating his vast new lands. They were jam-packed with Stone Age, Bronze Age and Roman monuments, and he had the money, time and labour to do the job thoroughly. His work is a model of scientific excavation: he dug, recorded and published meticulously. He wrote everything down. He considered every item he excavated to be important to his understanding of a site. 'Excavators as a rule,' he wrote, 'record only those things which appear important at the time. But fresh problems… keep arising and it can hardly fail to have escaped notice… that on turning back to old accounts in search of evidence, the points which would have been most valuable have been passed over from being thought uninteresting at the time. Every detail should therefore be recorded.'

It's the ground rules laid down by Pitt-Rivers that form the basis of modern archaeology.

Pitt-Rivers, father of modern archaeology (1827-1900).

So are you going to apply Pitt-Rivers's scrupulous modern scientific techniques when you excavate your garden? Of course you are. Not for you the slap-happy approach of the nineteenth-century gentry who'd plunge straight into the heart of your rockery in order to plunder its treasures.

So what kit will you need? You pick up your credit card and head down to your local garden centre. You buy a ball of string and some 6-inch nails, a sieve, a sharp spade, a bucket, and some plastic seed trays for putting your finds in. You'll also need a trowel – not a round-ended gardener's trowel or a long plasterer's one the size of a toucan's beak. You pick up a welded 4-inch bricklayer's pointing trowel: for the real archaeologist nothing else will do.

You're just about to go home again when a nagging doubt creeps into your mind. Once you start digging, how will you know when to stop? What signs are there to tell you when you've dug through all the archaeology and reached the untouched geology beneath? After all, you won't want to come to a halt a metre and a half down and miss out on the massive Roman temple a few centimetres below. On the other hand, you'll want to stop before you reach Australia. You're walking past a building site. Sometimes workmen are only too happy to discuss the geology of their site with passers-by. But you're out of luck. When you ask them, they look at you as though you're mad. So instead you go to your local library where they've got a big geological map of the area. It seems as though the geology (or the 'natural' as it's sometimes called) on which your street was built is gravel. You make a lot of notes then return home.

Back in your garden you've got to decide on the size of your hole. Your natural reaction is to dig the largest one possible, but remember you're going to need room at the surface to store the turf from your lawn. You'll also need space for your 'spoil-heap'. (You've just learnt your first archaeological term – a spoil-heap is the big pile of earth you shovel out of your hole.) You'll also want enough space to separate your topsoil from the subsoil so you can put it all back in the right order when you back-fill. On the other hand, you won't want to make your hole too small: it needs to be big enough for you to work in and see any archaeology at the bottom of it. So let's say your fictional hole in your fictional garden will be 2 metres by 1 metre. Except you won't be calling it a hole. From now on you'll use the proper archaeological term (see page 30).

In order to investigate the archaeology in your garden you're going to need to dig a trench. The next question is: where should you put it? The obvious answer is in the bit of the garden you're happy to trash, although don't dig under a tree because you may damage the roots and kill it. But there's a problem. You don't know where the services are laid. There's nothing more frustrating than digging down a metre or so only to discover you've hit a sewer pipe. If you could get hold of a Cat-Scan (the instrument used by builders to detect pipes and electric cables), it would save you a lot of trouble. But you've no idea where to find one, so you look at where the manhole covers and drains are located, and try to work out which way the services run. Nowadays it's standard practice to lay a plastic sheet inscribed 'Gas below' or words to that effect over newly installed services, so if you come down on one during your excavation, hard luck!

Using a Cat-Scan to locate pipes before an excavation begins.

You decide that one end of your trench is going into the vegetable patch, and the rest will be on the lawn. You mark it out so you can see where to dig. That's why you invested in the nails and string. You make sure the corners are crisp and right-angled. Pythagoras himself couldn't have done better. But you also need to know where your trench is in relation to your house. It may seem pretty obvious to you right now, but if you want to re-excavate in five years' time will you still remember its position? More importantly, suppose someone else wants to look at your work after you're dead and buried. There are museums all over the world full of potentially valuable finds, but whose original location is so vague they're virtually worthless. So you get out your tape measure, make the necessary measurements from the trench to your house, your fences and so on, and draw a scaled plan indicating where north is. Then underneath you write your name, your address and the date you made the plan. At some time in the future, if this plan's one of a hundred in a great sheaf of papers being researched by an archaeologist who's going to re-dig your area, it'll be useless unless it's clearly identifiable.

ARCHAEOLOGICAL HEALTH WARNING

Digging is a destructive process: in order to understand a site you have to take it apart and in effect destroy it. Even professional archaeologists don't embark on this process lightly. They have to be very careful and protective of what they quite rightly regard as a finite and limited number of archaeological sites. Only when there's a good reason to dig, and the expertise is available along with the resources to analyse and study all aspects, will an excavation be undertaken.

Your garden is your property and you have every right to dig it up (unless, of course, it's on a Scheduled Ancient Monument!). But if you do so, please excavate scrupulously in line with what we've written in this book, and if you find anything interesting, make sure you let someone experienced know about it.

Now, at long last, it's time to dig. You cut your grass into 30 x 30 centimetre squares with your spade – any bigger and the turfs may break when you're carrying them. As you pull one edge you find they're easy to lift. They come away from the soil below the root line at about 10 centimetres in depth. You stack them some way off, laying them grass to grass, and earth to earth.

You may think of your house as being in a town, but most urban land was farmland until fairly recently. So your garden was probably a field not so long ago, and a lot of the scattered finds will be debris that got into it during the manuring process. In addition the soil will have been continually ploughed by farmers and dug over by generations of gardeners, so the finds in your topsoil are unlikely to be in their original position.

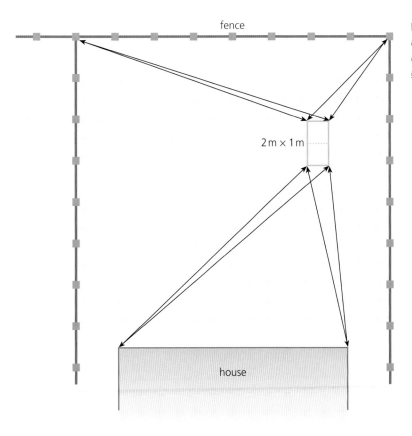

fence

2m × 1m

house

Fixing the position of your trench in relation to your house and the fences around your garden.

10 words for a hole

Eskimos have ninety words for snow. Archaeologists probably have even more to describe a hole. Here are a few of them.

1 A **TEST-PIT** is a very small exploratory hole, usually square (say, 1 x 1 or 2 x 2 metres). A number of test-pits are often dug on a site to get a snapshot of the archaeology below.

2 A **TRENCH** is a bigger hole, usually longer than it is wide, dug to investigate the archaeology.

3 An **AREA EXCAVATION** is a huge hole that spreads over a large part of an archaeological site.

4 A **SONDAGE** is a test-pit inside a trench or area excavation dug in order to see how deep the archaeology goes.

5 If archaeologists think they'll need a trench that will be so deep it could become dangerous, they have two choices. They can shore it up with acroprops and planks, but this obscures the archaeology in the sides of the trench. Or they can create a trench which is a series of steps (usually 1–1.5 metres high and wide). This is called a **STEPPED TRENCH.**

But archaeologists have to deal with other sorts of holes besides the ones they dig themselves. They also uncover evidence of holes dug by other people in the past.

6 For instance there's the **POST-HOLE.** A small patch of different coloured or textured earth in a trench is a clue that a hole was once dug there to support a wooden post.

7 A smaller patch of different coloured earth, where a stake has been hammered into the ground, is known predictably as a **STAKE-HOLE.**

8 Another common hole is the **PIT**. This is indicated by a much larger area of staining. Pits were dug for storage or to bury rubbish or human waste. They may also be all that's left of a kiln, hearth, oven or some other industrial practice.

9 A **DITCH** is a very long hole that was once dug as a boundary or a defence, or to drain water from a field. A ditch will usually appear in a trench as a dark strip of earth and, as you excavate further, the outline will show in the trench sides.
NB: If you want to have any archaeological credibility, don't confuse a ditch with the trench it's in.

10 A **ROBBER TRENCH** is another long hole. It's a bizarre name that doesn't have anything to do with masked men carrying sacks and coshes. People have always dug into the earth to 'rob' the stones and rubble from the foundations of demolished buildings, often leaving behind only the trench in which the wall once sat. This is what the monks of St Albans were doing a thousand years ago. Digging robber trenches isn't sinful, they're ancient examples of recycling (see page 69).

TEST-PIT

Test-pit revealing a fine cobbled surface (and a large root!). Note the blue plastic sheets, sieves and ranging rods (for scale).

TRENCH

Removing the topsoil with mattocks. Already a stony layer has been revealed with find spots marked with white labels

AREA EXCAVATION

An area excavation with a large number of features of different dates. Groups of excavators are examining various contexts. Note the tent for refreshments, finds, record processing and shelter, and the minibus for transporting the diggers.

DEEP HOLE

Below 1.4 metres, provision has to be made to stabilize the sides. Here, field archaeologist Phil Harding has put in boards, planks and acroprops.

DEEP TRENCH

A stepped trench. Note the wide steps either side of the deeper trench.

POST-HOLE

Post-hole dug into a stony surface with the post packed round with large stones. The context numbers tell us we are in Area B. The post-hole is Context 24, the packing is Context 13.

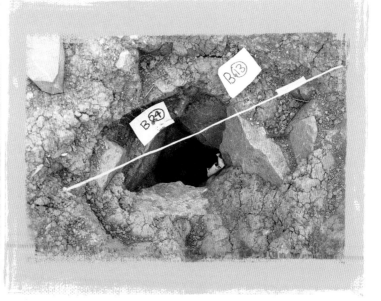

PIT

A small pit, half-sectioned, on a gravel site. Note the pit fill is slightly browner than the gravel. There is part of a prehistoric quern (milling) stone in the top.

PIT

A large pit, half-sectioned, in gravel. Note that the pit is browner than the surrounding gravel. In the section of the pit, holes can be seen where samples have been taken for environmental and dating evidence.

DITCH

A linear feature being excavated by field archaeologist Katie Hirst. She has left two sections across it for reference (note the string). The fill is redder than the surrounding material. More digging revealed a lot of charcoal and dark soil. This feature is probably the remnants of a slot with a burnt timber beam in it. It would have originally supported a wall or possibly a loom.

ROBBER TRENCH

Excavated robber trench at Athelney, Somerset. The wall which would have run under where archaeologist Kerry Ely is squatting has been totally removed down to the last stone.

Another culprit wrecking their historical integrity is the earthworm. These little blighters spend their entire lives yanking things up and down through the earth, and it's quite possible to find a piece of Roman bowl among the smashed pieces of a 1950s teacup simply because it's been brought to the surface by a particularly muscle-bound worm.

Because you can't accurately date your topsoil and it's all a consistent colour and texture, you realize it can be carefully removed. (If you'd found any part that was a different colour or odd in some way you'd have left it to be dealt with later.)

You use a spade and your new trowel and bucket to shift the earth. You work systematically from one end of your trench to the other, then put spadefuls of the soil into your sieve and work it through the mesh looking for finds. You note which part of the trench each spadeful came from. You need to know roughly where the finds are located in case there's a concentration of metalwork or pottery in one particular area which will provide a clue for later investigation. You sieve systematically along the trench. You've already caught a glimpse of the finds you're likely to discover in the topsoil – the glass, the buttons, the Dinky toy, the pottery, and the brick and slate. You put them in one of your newly purchased seed trays and label it Trench 1. On a big site

The build up of layers on an archaeological site. Each building has its demolished predecessor beneath it.

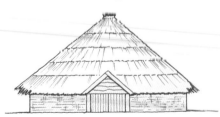
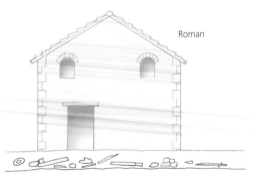

Prehistoric

Roman

archaeologists would also write the site code on it, but you haven't got one so you simply add your address and the date.

You need to establish where the topsoil comes to an end, so you can work out when you're down onto the next layer of archaeology. Complex sites, particularly urban ones, are created when buildings are constructed, demolished and levelled, then more buildings are constructed on top, then they're knocked down and flattened, and often this cycle continues uninterrupted for hundreds of years. This process has left its mark. You find layer upon layer of various coloured and textured earths peppered with differing amounts of stone, gravel, sand and clay – not to mention archaeological finds. The knack of the archaeologist is to recognize the subtle changes between these layers, every one of which can represent a different phase of human activity or building. Identifying these is a highly specialized skill, and you're not going to learn it overnight, but even on your first dig you're able to tell the difference between the dark rich topsoil and the layer beneath.

You take off all the topsoil until you reveal a much lighter orangey level throughout the whole trench. The layer you've removed is called a context – in other words it represents one phase of human activity. Archaeologists rather unimaginatively call the first level 'Context 1'. You fill in a context sheet describing

Anglo-Saxon

Medieval

A context sheet.

SITE CODE:		TRENCH:	CATEGORY: cut ☐ layer ☐ fill ☐ structure ☐	CONTEXT NO:

DEPOSIT

1. Colour	
2. Composition	
3. Compaction	cemented ☐ compact ☐ firm ☐ soft ☐ friable ☐
4. Coarse components	
5. Horizon clarity	sharp ☐ clear ☐ diffuse ☐
6. Contamination risk	low ☐ medium ☐ high ☐
7. Methods and conditions	JCB ☐ mattock ☐ trowel ☐ fine tools ☐
8. Other comments	

CUT

1. Shape in plan	rectangular ☐ circular ☐ sub-circular ☐ sub-rectangular ☐ linear ☐
2. Orientation	N-S ☐ W-E ☐ NE-SW ☐ NW-SE ☐ angle ☐
3. Sides	convex ☐ concave ☐ straight ☐
4. Base	flat ☐ sloping ☐ pointed ☐ tapered ☐
5. Feature clarity	sharp ☐ clear ☐ diffuse ☐
6. Methods and conditions	JCB ☐ mattock ☐ trowel ☐ fine tools ☐
7. Other comments	

Dimensions	Length:	Wdth :	Hght / Dpth:
	Top:	Base:	Diameter:

Stratigraphic Matrix

Earlier than ...	Physical relationships	Later than ...
Covered by:	Contemporary with ...	Cut by:
Filled by:	Part of:	Fill of:
Cut by:	Includes:	Cuts:
Butted by:	Same as:	Butts:

Finds Brick Bone Flint Glass CBM Metal Pot Slate Tile Wood None Other
☐ ☐ ☐ ☐ ☐ ☐ ☐ ☐ ☐ ☐ ☐ ☐

Volume dry sieved:	Provisional context date:					Photographs:	
	Mesolithic ☐	Bronze Age ☐	Roman ☐	Medieval ☐	Modern ☐	Colour slide:	☐
litres	Neolithic ☐	Iron Age ☐	Early medieval ☐	Post-medieval ☐	Unknown ☐	Black and white:	☐
Provisional context interpretation:							

what it is and what's in it. You never realized there was so much writing and recording involved in being an archaeologist, but this isn't unnecessary bureaucracy. As the dig progresses you'll see how vital the relationships between the various contexts are, and why you need to record them.

Now it's time to stretch your legs and wash your finds. Archaeologists tend to carry bundles of old toothbrushes round with them because they're ideal for washing fiddly little objects. You set the metal finds to one side, and all the rest from Context 1 are given a wash – gently, to avoid damaging the surfaces. You leave them to dry, remembering to leave a label with a context number by each group of finds. Drying may take a long time because by now your finds could well contain a lot of moisture. You can lay them in the sun on newspaper or on old egg boxes. Alternatively you can leave them in the airing cupboard or under the bed – where they can stay until they've completely dried out or until your partner threatens to throw them out of the window.

Later you'll put them into resealable polythene bags. Strong ones with white strips for writing on are best. It's vital that these bags are properly labelled. They may get wet or dirty or both, and could be manhandled for months before they're properly examined. So you have to make sure you label them with a waterproof pen and that your writing's legible. If you discover a coin, brooch or similar small find (archaeologists of course classify these as 'small finds'), bag or box it separately, and surround it with bubble-wrap so it's safe until a conservator decides how best to store it in the long term. Each label must have the name of the site on it, the date it was excavated, the number of the trench and the context number.

Is this emphasis on labelling and recording really necessary? Think Hercule Poirot. Every fingerprint and every hair he discovers is vital to his ability to solve the crime. Likewise every one of your finds is a clue to assist future archaeologists. Give them a break: bag and label your finds properly.

A line of diggers at Castle Howard in Yorkshire. They're cleaning the surface of a trench to reveal slight traces of peasant houses and a medieval road. Brownish clay is the main material here but there are discrete concentrations of stones where the buildings once were. The spoil is being removed with a shovel onto the spoil-heap behind.

A pocket guide to recording

We may be in danger of driving readers mad with constant references to recording. So from now on, if we don't mention this procedure at every stage of the excavation, don't assume recording of one sort or another isn't required. It is!

CONTEXT SHEETS *must be filled in continuously. As different layers, features and archaeological events such as post-holes, walls and graves are revealed, each one is given a separate context number and a detailed sheet is filled in. If, for example, a post-hole is being described, its size and depth will be recorded, along with a detailed description of the fill, including its colour, if it's sandy or clay-like, full of pebbles or charcoal, tightly packed or loose with voids. Any associated finds will be described, as well as any other details that might help in its interpretation. The sheets will also record the relationship between one context and another – 'below the orange layer', 'cut by the post-hole', 'overlain by the grey layer' and so on. They'll note details of any samples that have been taken, and any photos will be included, as well as a description of the conditions at the time of excavation and the name of the archaeologists who did the work. Context sheets are the basic record about a site, and there's space on them for the excavators to add their own personal touch by writing down their interpretation of the contexts they're describing.*

At every stage of a dig a **PLAN** *is made to show the location of contexts and features. To make these plans accurate, certain basic surveying skills are required, because each plan needs to be 'tied in' to its surroundings, so the excavation can be related to the local environment with the help of a large-scale Ordnance Survey map. Each plan has to have a title, a number, a north sign, a scale, the name of the recorder, and the date of the drawing. It will usually be drawn on a scale of 1:20. Detailed areas of stones, skeletons, etc are drawn by laying a planning frame over the feature and drawing it a square at a time (see picture on page 44).*

A **SECTION DRAWING** *is a picture of a vertical slice through part of a site to show what layers are found where. Sections are drawn wherever they're exposed, through the sides of trenches, through walls, across ditches and robber trenches or through half of a pit or post hole to show their relationship with one another. Sections are usually drawn at a scale of 1:10. As with a plan, each drawing will have a title, context numbers, orientation, a scale, the name of the recorder and the date. It should also be annotated to help clarify the description of the layers.*

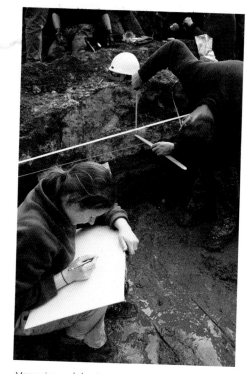

Measuring and drawing contexts in a section at Castleford, Yorkshire.

Each stage should be photographed. These photographs should principally be of the excavation rather than the excavators, though the latter are sometimes of interest! Both black and white prints and colour slides should be taken, using a good quality single-lens reflex camera or digital camera. Once again, each picture should have a metric scale, a north sign, the context numbers, the site code and the date. This information is often written on a small chalkboard or equivalent, which is then placed in the picture. As well as identifying what's being photographed, this will also help show which way round the slide should be viewed (see picture on page 93).

There should be cross-referencing between all the records of the features, find spots and contexts of a site. The plan will have the contexts marked on it, the context records will have the relevant plan numbers on them and both will record the section drawings. The slides and photographs will be properly labelled and numbered. Much of this has to be done while the site is being excavated, and it must be completed immediately after the excavation when the archive of the site is being prepared. Once all the specialists' reports have been completed, and the excavation written up for publication, the main archive, which will include all this material plus the finds, will be deposited in a museum (provided one has agreed to take it!). It will then be available for anyone in future generations to come and examine it or carry out further work.

Make sure to keep a separate copy as a security precaution. Reports can get lost, burnt, stolen or have coffee poured all over them.

Now back to your site. You've taken all the topsoil off your trench, next it's time to get the new surface clean. For an archaeologist, cleaning doesn't involve water, a mop or Ajax. You simply take off a thin layer of the surface with the side of your trowel so that the surface is even and there's no loose soil knocking about. You work from one end of the trench to the other. This isn't to make it look pretty, it's so you can spot potential clues. A lot of archaeology isn't solid finds that you can dig up and put in a museum. It's stains in the soil, the ghosts of past human activity, and such subtle differences can be detected only if the surface is clean and consistent.

Having done the cleaning, you look carefully at the result. You can see that the new surface is totally different from the topsoil. Your new orangey layer is dotted with pebbles. From now on we'll call this 'Context 2', and you can start filling in a context sheet for it and drawing it. It'd be a good idea to take a photo of it too. There are a number of pieces of pottery here which aren't like the glazed material that was in the topsoil. This stuff is unglazed, it's red and black and has a crumbly, biscuity feel to it. It may not look very attractive, but it could be old. You don't remove these pieces yet. They're part of the orangey layer below. Remove them only when you take the whole orangey layer out.

Recording the position of the circular feature.

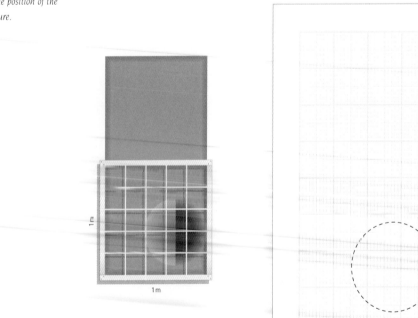

1 m

1 m

You step back and look at your surface again. In order to get sufficiently far away from it you get a ladder from the garage. But then you have an even better idea. You take your boots off, go indoors, climb upstairs, and look out your bedroom window. You feel slightly silly, but even the greatest archaeologists work this way. At first the whole surface looks confused. You can't work out the difference between the shadows and the various colours of the soil. But once the sun goes in, everything becomes clear. Close up, the whole surface looked pretty uniform, but now you can see that in one corner of the trench there's a circular shadow about half a metre across. What could it be? There are some quite big stones in it and the centre seems slightly darker than the rest.

Congratulations! You've discovered your first archaeological feature. You've now taken your first step on the road to becoming an archaeologist. But what could it be? A hearth? A pit? Or is it just where your dog buried a bone last week?

Well, no, it can't be modern, because when you went through the topsoil there was no sign that the turf and flower bed had been disturbed. This feature only started at the top of Context 2, so it must be related to Context 2 and not the layers above it. We'll call this feature 'Context 3', and, before you start to explore it, you draw the trench, making your picture large enough to include all the details. Then you survey in the feature located in the corner.

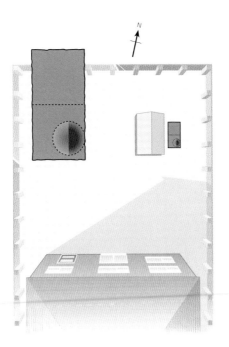

High view of your trench, next to the garden shed.

Part of a filled-in context sheet.

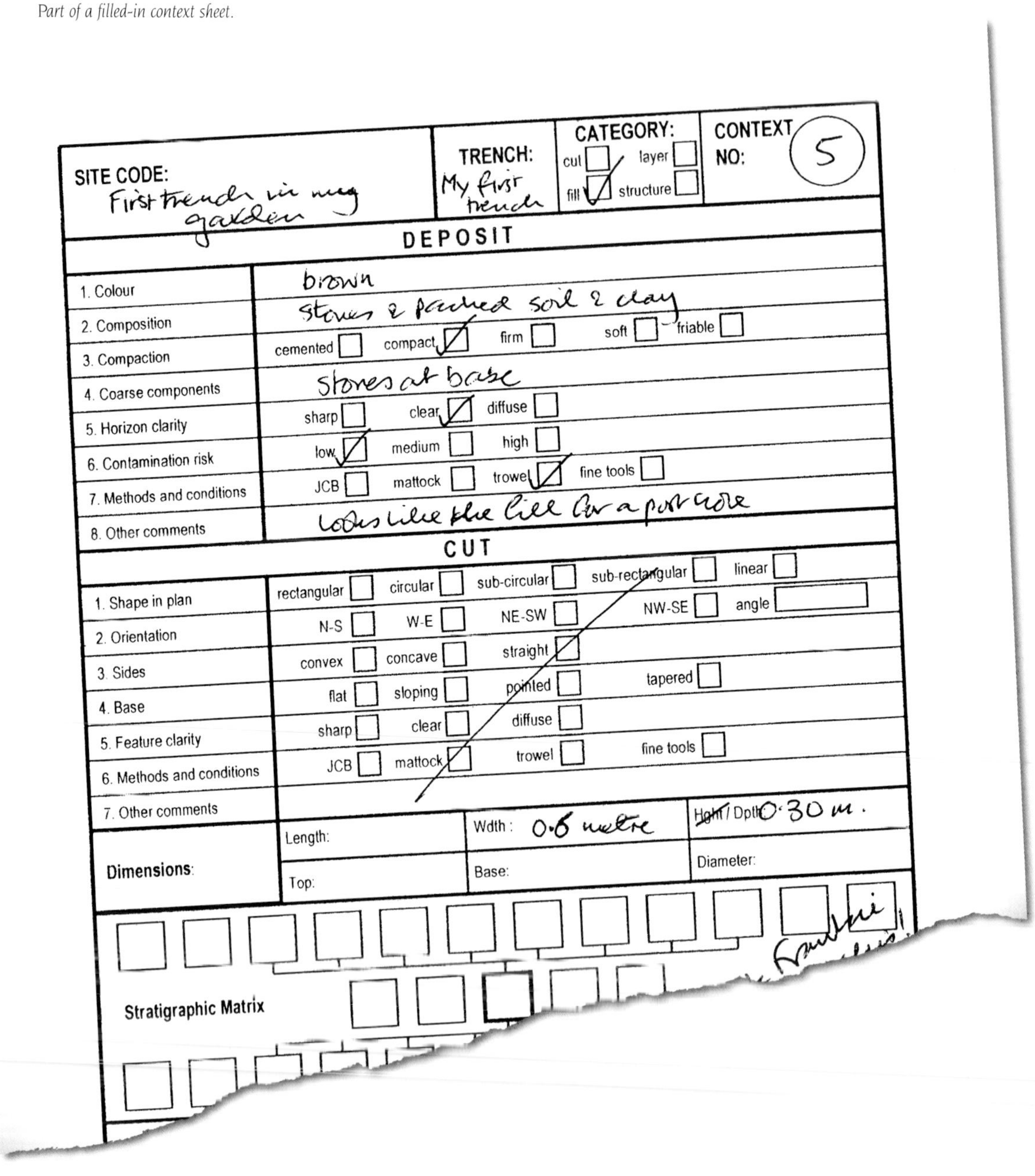

SITE CODE: *First trench in my garden*	TRENCH: *My first trench*	CATEGORY: cut ☐ layer ☐ fill ☑ structure ☐	CONTEXT NO: ⑤

DEPOSIT

1. Colour	brown
2. Composition	Stones & packed soil & clay
3. Compaction	cemented ☐ compact ☑ firm ☐ soft ☐ friable ☐
4. Coarse components	Stones at base
5. Horizon clarity	sharp ☐ clear ☑ diffuse ☐
6. Contamination risk	low ☑ medium ☐ high ☐
7. Methods and conditions	JCB ☐ mattock ☐ trowel ☑ fine tools ☐
8. Other comments	Looks like the fill for a post hole

CUT

1. Shape in plan	rectangular ☐ circular ☐ sub-circular ☐ sub-rectangular ☐ linear ☐
2. Orientation	N-S ☐ W-E ☐ NE-SW ☐ NW-SE ☐ angle ☐
3. Sides	convex ☐ concave ☐ straight ☑
4. Base	flat ☐ sloping ☐ pointed ☐ tapered ☐
5. Feature clarity	sharp ☐ clear ☐ diffuse ☐
6. Methods and conditions	JCB ☐ mattock ☐ trowel ☐ fine tools ☐
7. Other comments	

Dimensions:	Length:	Wdth: 0·6 metre	Hght / Dpth 0·30 m.
	Top:	Base:	Diameter:

Stratigraphic Matrix

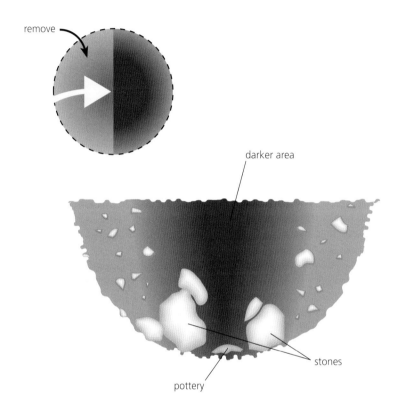

remove

darker area

stones

pottery

To find out what your feature is, you divide the circular stain in two with your string and 6-inch nails. Then you carefully take the earth out from one half of it with your trowel. When you dissect it, you can see a sectioned face. It's a bit like cutting a trifle in half. If you've ever done this to while away a long, rainy Sunday afternoon, you'll know that when you look at the section, you can see if the custard goes all the way through or whether it's interrupted by layers of cherries, jelly, jam and soggy biscuit. In a similar way an archaeological section can tell you about the layers in a feature.

This sectioning is interesting stuff, but don't dig too fast. You work your way down uniformly, and dig outwards as well as down in order to define the outside edges of the feature where the colour of the earth changes. You remove the earth gently and avoid over-digging into the next layer or the sides. As long as the material you're taking out of your hole looks the same, you can keep digging. Once you're at the bottom and it's cleaned, you take a long cool look at it. You can see another piece of grotty grey pottery like the stuff you found on the surface of Context 2. But this piece is sitting right at the bottom of your feature about 30 centimetres down, on a layer of gravelly material. Could this gravel be the basic geology of the area? You look at the notes you took in the library. It certainly seems like it.

You draw and photograph the section. As you do so, you look at the half of the feature you haven't removed. The middle of it is darker than the rest and stone-free. What could it be?

What clues have you got? It appears that at some time in history someone dug a hole half a metre wide and 30 centimetres deep. They dropped a piece of pottery in it, presumably by accident. This pottery is the same type as the bits in the orange layer of Context 2. So it probably belongs to the same period, and as it's in the bottom of the hole, the chances are that the hole was dug in the same period as your pottery was used. If you can date the pottery, you can date the hole to the same period or later.

But what was the hole originally for? Something that has now rotted away was once placed in it, and, in order to support this something, stones were put in it, and clay and other material were rammed around it. It looks like you've found a post-hole. If people want to put up a fence the first thing they do is to dig post-holes. But let's think big. This may not be a fence. It could be one of the posts of a house or a barn or something even bigger. Maybe it's a huge feasting hall! Looks like you've put your trench in the right place. Well done! Time to go inside for a tea-break.

Your first find wasn't very dramatic, was it? But even though your little sherd of pottery looks like nothing more than a dirty lump of grey dog biscuit, it's actually jam-packed full of clues. Try an experiment. Take a final swig from your mug of tea, then smash it on the floor. Pick up one of the little pieces, and look at its broken edges. The pottery is fine and even in texture and made of white clay. Compare it with your ancient fragment. The older bit's rougher and grittier. It's got little lumps of stone and holes in it, and it varies in colour – red on one side and black on the other.

The outside of your mug is patterned and has got a shiny glazed surface, but your old piece isn't glazed, has no obvious pattern, and the surface is so pimply it looks as though it's had a mild attack of acne.

You're well into this experiment now. You scrabble about under the coffee table and collect up more bits of your mug. They're a variety of different shapes. There are pieces of rim with rounded edges, bits of the handle, L-shaped fragments that show where the side originally joined the base, and bits of the body of the mug with a gentle curve to them.

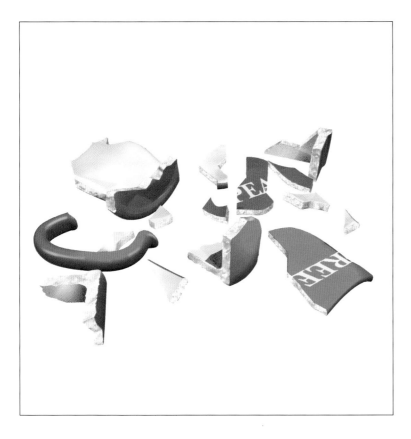

You look at the piece you dug up. You can see that it's curved too, so you should be able to get some idea of the diameter of the rim of the original vessel. You need a compass. You run round to Mrs Gater next-door-but-one, and while she's rummaging through her son Colin's pencil-case you tell her what you've been doing. She's almost as enthusiastic as you are. She's fascinated by the history of this area and has always wanted to know if there's anything interesting buried in the back gardens. Not only does she find you a compass, she also lends you Colin's metal detector which she bought him last Christmas but which he's never even taken out of the box.

You go back home and draw a series of circles on a sheet of paper. You want to compare them with the curve on your piece of pot so you can tell how big the pot originally was. After a lot of fiddling, you're pretty sure it would have been about 20 centimetres across at the rim. The curve also tells you which is the outside and which is the inside. The outside is much more blackened than the inside, so it could well have been part of a cooking pot charred from sitting on the fire.

10cm
20cm
30cm
diameter

How fragments of pottery can tell us the form of the original vessel.

You may think this is a lot of evidence from one small fragment, but there's much more. Three edges of your piece are broken, but the fourth edge is flattened and smooth. There's only one part of a pot that has a smooth edge like this – the rim. So you now know that this edge is the top. You can also see that the bottom of your piece begins to flare out – which indicates that the body of the vessel was wider than its rim, possibly up to 30 centimetres in diameter judging by the angle. Although it's got no glaze or pattern on it, you can make out a series of vague horizontal lines where it was originally made on a potter's wheel, and there's a streakiness where the potter wiped the pot. There's even a fingermark of the person who made it.

You get a magnifying glass and take another look at the broken edges of your pot. There are bits of grit in it.

Anyone who's ever tried to make a pot out of pure clay knows it doesn't work – when you heat it in the kiln, it cracks or even explodes. You need an additive that will strengthen the clay and allow it to dry out more evenly (what potters call a temper or filler). Since pots were first made in Britain about 6,000 years ago, potters have mixed a variety of different additives with their clay – crushed stone, shell, bone, flint, sand or in some cases chopped-up straw or grass. Different materials were used at different times and in different places, so the temper can be a superb dating clue. Potters often wandered from village to village and from town to town making and selling their wares, but they seldom carried their raw materials with them. Clay and filler were so common and so heavy that the travelling potters acquired them locally. So if you find a pot with filler in it that isn't made from something local, it's almost certain that it arrived where it is now because it was traded. A specialist will be able to tell you the source of the grit in your pot, and consequently where it was probably made.

So putting all the evidence together, you now know that you've got a piece of cooking pot that was made on a potter's wheel in a specific place which can be identified and was sold to someone around here. You've even got the potter's fingerprint. But how can you work out how old it is? For that matter, how do archaeologists know the age of anything from the past?

Late Saxon pottery from Shapwick, Somerset. Rough, dog-biscuit-like sherds with voids and quartz crystals.

English stone ware from 1750 to 1900, some with letters of a company or indications of contents. These were used as general purpose containers before plastic became available.

The easiest things to date are those that have a date on them! But almost as good are those finds which we know were made at a particular time. During the eighteenth and nineteenth centuries, antiquarians almost always had a classical education, so they would have been pretty familiar with Greek and Roman history. In particular, they'd have known the dates of the Roman emperors. These emperors minted different coins throughout their reigns which were then distributed across the Roman empire. Fifteen hundred years later the same coins were turning up in the archaeology that the antiquarians were starting to discover. The coins didn't have dates on them but the antiquarians were able to identify which emperor was which by the shape of the nose, the length of the beard, even the different lettering which was used round the edges of the coins. And when these coins of known date were found next to pottery and other objects, they deduced that the finds were roughly the same age as the coins.

It was soon realized that this handy coin-dating evidence was also indispensable for dating in the Anglo-Saxon and medieval periods, and it continued to be relied on by archaeologists as the sole way of dating finds right up to the 1960s. But even when you get what appears to be an accurate date from a coin, you need to be sceptical. If you threw your broken mug into the garden it might end up near a two pence piece with the date 1982 on it. The old assumption would have been that the mug and the money were of the same date. This is approximately true, but actually it's two decades out. And suppose you found the same coin next to a broken bowl from the coronation of Queen Victoria which had been in your family since the 1830s, but which you broke during a small dispute with your partner? Using only the evidence obtained from the coin, the date would be nearly 200 years out.

Coin-dating wasn't possible in the prehistoric layers below the Roman ones, which the Victorians called the 'Ancient British' levels. For these levels they tried to work out how old a site was from a series of calculated guesses about how long 'Ancient British' objects had been in use. For instance, they calculated that a particular type of stone axe might have been used for a thousand years, or a particular Bronze Age arrowhead for 500 years.

Caligula
(37-41)

Nero
(54-68)

Hadrian
(117-138)

Antoninus
(138-161)

Carausius
(287-293)

Soft-drink containers have changed dramatically over the last 100 years or so.

Then in the late nineteenth century Pitt-Rivers developed a brand-new dating method that was highly appropriate for these prehistoric layers. He began comparing the shape and complexity of man-made objects. Most objects change over the years as technologies develop and more sophisticated ways of making things are discovered. Think of the history of the portable radio. The first ones were made of Bakelite and were so heavy you could hardly carry them from your kitchen to your sitting room. With the invention of the transistor they became much lighter. Microchips gave us the Walkman with its featherlight earphones, and the new technology of WAP telephones with built-in radio receivers has sent designers scurrying off to change the shape of radios all over again. Pitt-Rivers delved into his collection of tools and weapons, laid them out, and arranged them in order. He assumed that they'd evolved just as birds, fish and human beings had evolved. So the most crudely made ones were the oldest, and the more sophisticated ones came later.

This principle ('typology', as it's known) is still in use today. The piece of pottery from the garden is cruder and less sophisticated than your teacup. It's therefore assumed to be much older.

But typology is rife with problems. It's based on the assumption that artefacts always start out simple and get more sophisticated. But this isn't necessarily true. For instance, late Bronze Age stone scrapers aren't nearly as well made as Stone Age ones, even though they were made thousands of years later. This is because, as metal blades become more common, people didn't bother to work stone in such a complex way.

Another problem is that while it's true that utensils made for the elite in a society tend to develop quite quickly, these changes don't occur nearly as fast in common-or-garden objects used by ordinary people. In the eighteenth century the fashion for drinking tea meant that wealthy landowners were suddenly desperate to acquire new tea-sets made of porcelain and bone china, and the top end of the pottery industry was revolutionized almost overnight. But at the same time the workers on those landowners' estates were still drinking from cups that looked not unlike those used in the Middle Ages or even by the Anglo-Saxons.

So if you found a piece of pottery today that had been owned by an eighteenth-century farm-worker, and another piece from an eighteenth-century aristocrat's teacup, then using only typology you'd assume they were from wildly different periods of time, even though in fact they were simply owned by people from two different social classes.

Yet another problem is that even though you may have managed to get the sequence of archaeological events right, if you don't know the date of any of the individual objects then all you've got is relative dating between them. They 'float' in time until you can anchor them to a real date by discovering some other piece of evidence. Nevertheless, both coin dating and typology were great steps forward in understanding how old things were.

The development of geology added another principle. Generally, the lower in a sequence an artefact was found, the older it was, the higher the newer. Roman pottery was almost certain to be found below Saxon pottery, while Saxon would be below Norman, and Norman would be below medieval. So the study of layers ('stratification' is the archaeological term) became a key dating tool.

And essentially this was as good as dating got until the 1960s. Until then, the age of an object was almost always a major obsession with archaeologists because it was so difficult to ascertain. But then new technologies arrived on the scene that completely transformed the whole discipline.

Today, by using contemporary techniques, specialists would be able to say quite confidently that your piece of pot is not only medieval, but that it was made between AD 1100 and 1200, and that consequently your post-hole was dug by the year 1200 or later. This more precise kind of dating wouldn't have been possible forty years ago, and when scientists look at the rest of the finds on your site, they'll be able to tell you other things about it that Pitt-Rivers could only have dreamed of.

CHAPTER 5

Before you get back to serious digging, is there anything more you can learn about the story of your site from the work you've done so far? The answer is yes. You can use the sides of the post-hole as a window through which you can see what's going on below the main level of the trench. You get down on your hands and knees and have a look. Under the orangey layer (Context 2), which you think is medieval because of the bits of pot you've seen in it, there's a really dark, almost black layer of peaty soil, and below that a more yellowy layer. Finally, below that is the natural gravel.

Now you've got some idea of how deep each context will be, you feel confident enough to take off the whole orange medieval layer (Context 2) by hand with your trowel. As you remove it, you keep the odd bits of medieval pottery and animal bone that are turning up. You continue until there's no more of that layer left and the whole trench has turned peaty-black. You're now at the top of the next layer, which is Context 6. Why isn't it Context 3? Take a look at the diagram.

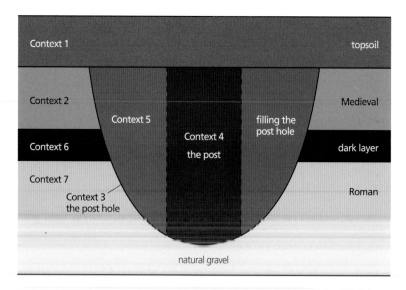

Context 1	topsoil
Context 2	Medieval
Context 5	filling the post hole
Context 6	Context 4 the post	dark layer
Context 7	Roman
Context 3 the post hole	natural gravel

Why the dark layer isn't Context 3.

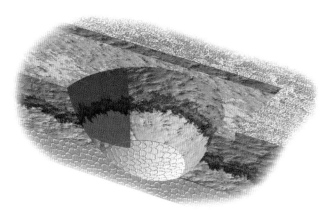

Context 3 – digging the post-hole.

Context 4 – setting up the post.

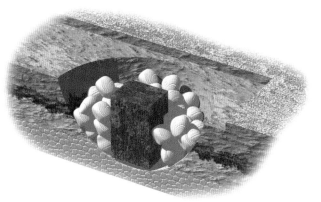

Context 5 – filling the post-hole.

When you've cleaned it up, you see there are no distinguishing features in it at all – no finds, no post-holes, no burnt areas, no darker or lighter areas. If you didn't know better you might think you'd come down onto natural earth, untouched by human activity, but you can see from the sides of your post-hole that the layer is only about 10 centimetres thick. Because you've no other clues about what's going on in it, you unpack Colin's metal detector and run it over the surface. This could be an Anglo-Saxon layer. It is after all under the medieval one. How will you know? In most parts of Britain you don't find much Anglo-Saxon pottery, but if you're lucky you might turn up a metal Anglo-Saxon strap end or belt buckle.

Result! You've got a signal!

You put a marker in to fix the spot and then you carefully remove Context 6. As it hasn't got any features in it, you can take the earth off with your trowel in four-centimetre layers. This should ensure that it's done reasonably quickly but that you'll spot any finds or features that may be lurking there. You can't see any, but you take a couple of half-bucket sized samples of earth, put them in plastic bags and label them. It may be that later on, if it can be dated, this black stuff will contain some useful environmental information.

When you get to the area where Colin's metal detector gave you a reading, you work a bit more gingerly. If there is a find down there, it'll be very old and could be in pretty poor condition.

But there doesn't seem to be anything at all, just uniform black earth. Maybe the metal detector's faulty. Should you stop trowelling and check to see if the guarantee's still in the box? No, the detector's fine. There's something down there after all. It's a coin. You carefully lift it. It certainly looks old. It's rather beautiful actually. Tiny and silver.

Coin of King Offa.

Now you can see it's got a face on it, and you can make out a name too – Offa Rex. It's from the reign of King Offa. He was the King of Mercia in central England from AD 757 to 796. This is great dating evidence. It looks as if this dark layer is well and truly from the Anglo-Saxon period.

By the way, because it's silver, it would be a good idea to tell your local Portable Antiquities Officer, who you'll be able to contact via your nearest museum or Sites and Monuments Records Office (see page 65). Then give yourself a pat on the back. Most coins, apart from those found on archaeological sites, are simply ripped out of the soil by their finders as trophies. They disappear into private collections without having been properly recorded, so are completely useless, providing no information at all for historians

original trench

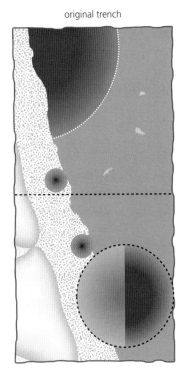

and archaeologists. But as you've worked so carefully, you know exactly how your coin relates to what's around it, and it can be fitted into the story, not only of your back garden, but of your whole locality.

When you've surveyed the position and depth of your coin, you carry on emptying out Context 6 until you're down on to the yellowy layer that you could see in the side of the post-hole. You get a bit frustrated by having to fill in so many context sheets, but at least this forces you to slow down and look hard at the relationship between the layers and to think about what they might mean.

You look at the new surface very carefully. It's a patchwork of different shades of yellow and brown clay. When you clean it up, several things immediately become obvious. There are two black blotches in it which seem to contain material of exactly the same colour and consistency as the black material you've just taken off. Could these be more post-holes or stake-holes from Anglo-Saxon times? You also seem to have lots of bits of stone showing across one side of your trench and some of them have got chalky, crumbly bits around them. At one end of the trench there's a clay area with bits of pottery embedded into it. In one corner there's an area of dark soggy stain which doesn't seem to crop up anywhere else, and there's also a tiny piece of very interesting-looking red stone about 1 centimetre square which definitely looks man-made. The words 'Roman' and 'mosaic' spring to mind, but you immediately suppress them. There's no point getting too excited.

Then you get hit by a wave of panic. So many features! This is real archaeology. Have you bitten off more than you can chew? Maybe this site is too complicated for you to cope with. By excavating, are you likely to wreck the archaeology? Once you've taken it apart, it's gone for ever – you can't put it back together again. What an awesome responsibility. Perhaps you should have taken up stamp collecting or knitting instead, or learnt to use a skateboard.

A tiny voice inside you tells you to stay cool. You take a few deep breaths. Archaeology is about looking and thinking, and sorting out the interrelationship between various features by carefully removing them. Just carry on with the job, but first think about what may be down there. The stones could be part of a wall, and the chalky stuff may be early cement or mortar. The fact that the clay layer has got bits of pot in it is extremely good news. With luck, you'll be able to date it. You know it's below the Anglo-Saxon layer. Maybe there really is something Roman down there.

You plan the feature, then section the black holes that you think may be Anglo-Saxon.

One is very shallow and has stone at the bottom. It doesn't appear to tell you much at all. But you record it just in case. Then you move on to the second one. It's about 10 centimetres deep and in the side of it there's a lot of the crumbly, chalky material you've seen near the stones.

Now you give the rest of the trench floor another good clean. You take about half a centimetre off all over it to show up the different colours and textures. You can see that you were right. The bits of pottery in the clay are definitely big Roman sherds. The black pieces are burnished ware, made in Dorset and exported over the whole of Roman Britain. There are bits of locally made grey wares, and most excitingly a piece of shinier, smoother, finer, red pottery. This is Samian ware, imported from Gaul in the first and second centuries AD. The local ware is hand made stuff, but this Samian pottery was factory-produced in vast quantities, and is found all over Western Europe. It implies that your site isn't just a run-of-the-mill farm. You could have the broken dinner service of someone of high status.

Enough sherds of this black-burnished cooking pot survive to give us the complete base, the profile of the side and indications of the rim. This type of pottery was some of the most common in Britain in the Roman period.

You've hit quite a problem. The pottery seems to be saying you've got a Roman site, and the two features in it (the possible wall and the darker area) could be Roman too. But your trench simply isn't big enough for you to get a good look at what these features actually are. In fact it's now nearly half a metre deep and so small you can hardly turn round in it. If you're going to be able to understand it, you'll have to make your trench bigger. Unfortunately, this will take you under your garden shed.

You've got two options. You can record everything, fill the trench in, hand in your finds and records, and concentrate on improving your skateboard technique, knowing you've already done a decent day's archaeology. Or else you can extend and say goodbye to your shed. It's a tough decision. What on earth are you going to do?

When you've destroyed the shed and carried the last remnants to Mrs Gater's skip, you get the number of the County Archaeological Department from the local council and phone to ask for advice. The person who answers sounds interested, but says your County Archaeologist is currently snowed under dealing with road schemes and large housing estate developments, and weighed down taking local councillors on tours of the town's archaeological sites, not to mention having to visit Grimsby in order to attend an important archaeological conference. So it'll be a few days before she can get back to you. In the meantime the department's happy for you to carry on, as long as you continue to be as careful as you've been so far.

Restored but otherwise almost complete Samian ware bowl. These pots were made in a mould from good quality red clay in factories in Gaul. They had a bright red slip surface over a variety of decorations or scenes.

How to find an archaeologist

There could be any of four different sorts of full-time archaeologist in your area.

There will probably be some sort of local authority archaeologist, either county or district, working for your council. They're often based in the planning department (sometimes called the 'property' or 'environment' department). Part of their job will be to maintain the County Sites and Monuments Record (SMR), though there may well be a separate archaeologist to look after this. They'll also advise the planning department on archaeological issues relating to planning applications.

There may be an archaeologist in your nearest museum. Their job is often to look after the local collections, put on displays and so on.

There could be a Portable Antiquities Officer based in the museum, or one who visits the museum regularly. Their job it is to liaise with people who find things, and especially to record finds made by metal detectorists.

There may be any number of commercial archaeological units operating in your region, though they could be based a long way away. They compete to secure contracts to undertake excavations which are needed before developments are allowed to go ahead.

So your first contact will probably be with the local authority archaeologist or someone in the museum. How do you find out about them? You can begin by looking in your telephone directory or in the Yellow Pages under 'archaeology', or ring the offices of your local council and ask for their archaeologist.

There's an association of local government archaeologists (ALGAO), who can be contacted on the internet or through the Country Archaeologist, Environment Dept, Hertfordshire County Council, County Hall, Hertford SG13 8DN. This address changes frequently depending on where the administrator is based; this is current for 2002.

The present address for the Society of Museum Archaeologists is: Andover Museum, 6 Church Close, Andover, Hampshire SP10 1DP.

The Institute of Field Archaeologists is a professional association concerned with maintaining standards and assessing levels of competence. It has a membership list and is based at the University of Reading.

Archaeologists working with the Portable Antiquities Scheme should be contacted through your county museum or via your County Archaeologist. The current address for more information about the scheme is; Resource Outreach Officer c/o Dept of Coins and Medals, British Museum, London WC1B 3DG. A leaflet explaining the scheme is available directly from the Department of Culture, Media and Sport by calling 020 7211 6200. Also available from the DCMS is a leaflet explaining the Treasure Act and the Treasure Act: Code of Practice handbook. Internet users can visit the Portable Antiquities website at: www.finds.org.uk

You begin to extend your trench. Originally it was 2 x 1 metres, now it'll be 2 x 2 metres. You approach your new area in the same way as you did the old one. You now know what the archaeology is likely to be… but there's one crucial difference. In Context 1 of your new extension you've got lots of house bricks, which until half an hour ago supported the floor of your demolished shed. In addition you've got all the debris that fell through the gaps in the floorboards over the last twenty-five years. You're not sure whether or not to clean and record the broken Phillips screwdriver, the tailplane of the Airfix Lancaster bomber kit, the chewed rubber bone and the yo-yo. But Pitt-Rivers would have done, so you do too. Then you take off, clean and record the same sequence of layers that was in the original trench. Fortunately there don't seem to be any archaeological complications, but you do find another medieval post-hole on your way down, as well as another two of the possibly Anglo-Saxon stake-holes. As you dig and record them, it crosses your mind that two post-holes might mean there was once a medieval building in your garden.

The extension contains a lot more stones and mortar, which appear to be following the same line as the stones you found previously. But in one corner there's a surprise. One of your Anglo-Saxon stake-holes has cut through a pinkish surface and there are two more little red squares sticking out of it. The words 'Roman mosaic' float up to the surface of your mind again, but this time you're not quite so excited. If you're only getting little fragments it's probable that any such floor was ripped up or damaged by ploughing at some time in the past.

You decide that from now on you'll treat the extension and your original trench as one. You clean the whole surface of the extended trench once again and now you can see that the lines of parallel stones are all that's left of a wall. Once it had two faces of stone and in the middle a core of rubble and chippings, all held together with mortar. Unfortunately the Anglo-Saxon stake-drivers cut through this wall, presumably not realizing it was there, in order to put up whatever it was that was erected in later centuries. You had a preview of this when you saw the stone at the bottom of your shallower stake-hole. Some sweating Anglo-Saxon obviously gave up on those particular stakes when he hit what he thought was solid rock.

As you draw it, you begin to see much more of the shape of your dark area. It now appears to be roughly circular and about a metre across. It may be a round pit but, whatever the feature is, the circle is broken by the wall you've found. Does this mean the wall was built partly over a circular pit (in which case the wall is later)? Or was a D-shaped pit built alongside the wall, which would indicate that the wall was already there when the feature was dug (i.e. the wall is earlier)?

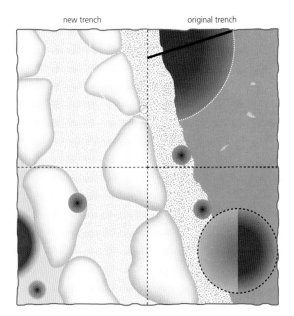

new trench   original trench

Plan of the extended trench. The black line at the top right is the section (see page 68).

How can you resolve this? As with your post-hole, indeed as with any features that are dug into earlier archaeology, the solution is to half-section the feature.

Because you want to know the relationship between the feature and the wall, you need to cut your half-section through it in such a way that this relationship is clearly visible. You also need to see the profile of the feature itself, so you can tell whether it really is a pit, or whether it's a ditch or something else.

So you take a line across it at right-angles to the wall, from the wall to the feature's outer edge. If this feature is circular, half of the circle is under the wall and another quarter is outside your original trench. This means you've only got a quarter to play with.

You can see almost immediately that there's a difference in the consistency of the material in the half-metre nearest to the wall compared with the dark gungy material in the rest of the feature. Nearer the wall it's stonier, grittier and with lumps of clay and mortar mixed in with the gungy stuff. You carefully remove the mysterious 'mortary' material. As you go down, more and more layers of stone are revealed; 30 centimetres down you've emptied your section. And you're rewarded with plenty of new information for your notebook.

A section of the pit, alongside the Roman wall.

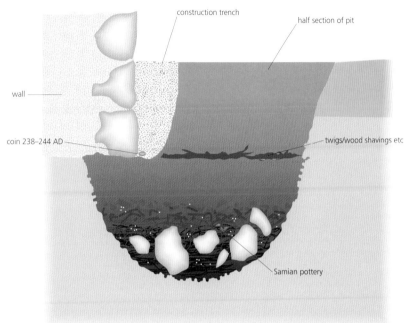

construction trench

half section of pit

wall

coin 238–244 AD

twigs/wood shavings etc

Samian pottery

First, you can now see that your mystery feature goes down only to the base of the wall. You know where the base is because you shove your trowel under the stones you've just revealed, and there are no more stones below them. The most likely explanation for this feature is that it's the construction trench that was dug when the wall was originally built. Builders still make houses in the same way today. Construction trenches are dug, the concrete and first courses of brick are laid, then the construction trench is filled in. The fact that the fill in your construction trench was mixed with so much of the dark gungy material implies that the trench was dug into the fill of the so-called pit. So the construction trench and therefore the wall are later than the pit.

Having seen that you've got a construction trench across your pit, you stand back and look at it in relation to the rest of the trench. That's when you get your second piece of information. You can now see that the 'mortary' area in your original trench is the continuing line of this ancient construction trench. You'd never have known that from your initial excavation. This alone justifies your decision to extend.

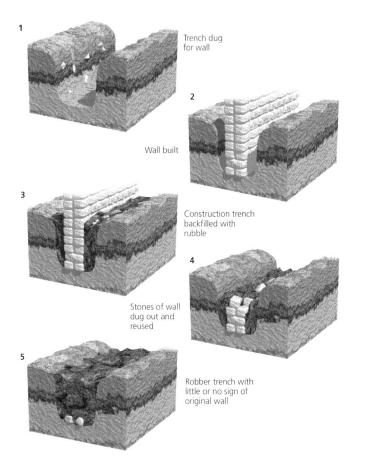

1 Trench dug for wall

2 Wall built

3 Construction trench backfilled with rubble

4 Stones of wall dug out and reused

5 Robber trench with little or no sign of original wall

There's another piece of information too, and this one's the best. You find it at the bottom of your newly discovered construction trench. It's another coin, it's silver, and it looks as though it's in almost mint condition. It's an 'antoninianus', and in AD 240 it would have bought you a decent lunch down at the tavern. You know the rough date because you can see the head of the emperor Gordian III on it, and he ruled between AD 238 and 244. The fact that this coin is right at the bottom of the construction trench, and right against the base stones of the wall, plus the fact that it's in near-mint condition, means that this wall can't have been built before AD 238. And as the coin isn't worn through use, it's probably not much after that date either. Once again the context of the coin is crucial. If it had been dug out willy-nilly without its context being recorded, this all-important dating information would have been lost forever. As it is, we now know that the 'yellowy' floor with Roman pottery in it was dug through, and is therefore earlier than, the construction trench. The wall, the trench and the 'yellowy' floor can all be put into a timeframe by your one coin.

You remove the fill from the rest of your pit, remembering to take a sample before you put the discarded material on the spoil-heap. As you go further down, the fill gets damper and darker. About half a metre down at a similar level to the base of the wall, you start to see recognizable leaves and twigs. There are even what seem to be the wing cases of beetles, wood shavings and little white snail shells. This stuff is clearly in a different league in terms of preservation to anything else you've seen on the site. Right at the bottom there are a couple of sherds of pottery. They're red and shiny, the kind that you know is called Samian. So it looks as though this pit is Roman too.

But what exactly is going on here? You've no idea. You realize you're not going to be able to interpret the pit feature on your own. You need an expert opinion.

Instead your attention shifts to the other side of the wall. You clean the pink plastery area carefully. This plaster goes right up to the wall, and there are even traces of it on the first course of stones. The two red little squares are stuck into its surface. Clearly they were once part of some sort of floor. By very careful cleaning you can just make out faint lines on the plaster. These indicate that more of these tiny tiles were once fixed to it. You're confident that you're dealing with an old mosaic floor made of thousands of little red 'tesserae' which was wrecked in later centuries.

So have you found a Roman villa? And is there an unspoiled mosaic floor still in existence somewhere round here? If there is, it could be in your next-door neighbour's garden. You and he can't stand each other. What are you going to do?

You go indoors, take some stiff liquid refreshment, and while you're mulling all this over, you phone the County Archaeologist again. This time you get to speak to her in person. You tell her what you've been doing and she promises to come round as soon as possible. She's particularly impressed that you took some environmental samples. You thought she'd want to see your tesserae, but it seems you were wrong. The things she can't wait to get her hands on are your snail shells!

What happened when?

There was no single dramatic moment in the dim and distant past when someone invented bronze and everybody threw away their stone axes. Nobody woke up in AD 1066 and decided they were fed up with being Early Medieval so from now on they'd be Late. The categories below are simply quick and easy ways of describing periods of human history. We've used them for convenience, but don't take them too seriously.

Before 8500 BC: *Palaeolithic or Old Stone Age*

8500–4000 BC: *Mesolithic or Middle Stone Age*

4000–2000 BC: *Neolithic or New Stone Age*

2000–700 BC: *Bronze Age*

700 BC to AD 43: *Iron Age*

AD 43–410: *Roman*

AD 410–1066: *Early medieval (including Anglo-Saxon)*

AD 1066–1500: *Late medieval*

AD 1500–1750: *Post-medieval*

AD 1750–1900: *Early modern*

AD 1900 onwards: *Modern*

CHAPTER 6

Fifty years ago there wasn't such a person as an environmental archaeologist. In fact archaeologists didn't bother much with the environment at all. Sites were dug, structures recorded and human artefacts analysed in pretty much the same way as archaeologists had done in the days of Pitt-Rivers. This meant that a lot of the rubbish that was dug up, like bones and shells and the fill from ancient ditches, was virtually ignored. It was thought of as part of nature, not as part of archaeology.

But then a sea-change occurred. A new generation of archaeologists trained after the Second World War began asking some very awkward questions:

'What's the point of digging up more things?'
'Maybe we should be digging sites in a different way.'
'Maybe we shouldn't be digging them at all?'
'What are we learning from all these excavations?'
'Have we found out all we can from the tons and tons of finds we've already got boxed up in the basements of our museums?'
'What do we know about the lives of the people who produced all this stuff?'
'What about the crops and animals they used?'
'What was their climate like?'
'Should we concentrate less on man-made objects, the "artefacts", and more on the natural background, the "ecofacts"?'

It was out of these difficult questions that modern archaeology arose. In order to try to answer them, these young archaeologists turned to other specialists for help. For many years Danish scientists had been trying to find out what their country had been like thousands of years ago and how it changed during the mysterious time that followed the end of the last Ice Age. They'd had the brainwave of looking at ancient pollen for clues. British archaeologists realized they could use the same kind of techniques to create a picture of what Ancient Britain had once been like. They plundered other biological techniques too and pretty quickly the science of environmental archaeology was born.

Above: *Geophysics in the back of a van may seem easy, but it can be profoundly frustrating!*

Left: *An early hand-built magnetometer.*

Below: *Before portable computers were developed, data plotters like this were the only way to read geophysical information in the field.*

Top: *The radiocarbon lab at Belfast, Northern Ireland.*

Bottom: *The newer Atomic Mass Spectrometry lab at the University of Oxford. The machinery is similar to the atom smashers used by theoretical physicists who look at the origin of the universe!*

A whole host of other new techniques began to influence archaeology. Geographers were developing complex mathematical ideas to explain why humans live in certain places and not others. These ideas were hijacked by archaeologists in order to work out why and how ancient people lived in the places that had been uncovered on their archaeological digs. They borrowed from sociology to learn about the power structures in ancient societies. Geology and metallurgy helped them look much more closely at their pottery and metal finds. Anthropology and economics were plundered to find out how trading patterns might have developed.

But one of the archaeologists' most frustrating problems wasn't interpreting what they'd found; it was trying to find what they were looking for. Many of them had wasted years poking around in the wrong place before they'd hit on their most important discoveries. Second World War boffins did away with all that wasted time. They developed a variety of remote sensing techniques such as radar and sonar. Archaeologists began to use them in the 1940s but the machines were cumbersome and heavy, and their cables and wires got hopelessly tangled. It wasn't until the 1980s, with the invention of microchips and lightweight computers, that remote sensing became more portable. It was suddenly possible to read what was going on under a field and to process the information in the back of a van. This was a godsend.

But the biggest archaeological breakthrough came from physics, and in particular from Carbon 14.

Living things take in particles of radioactive Carbon 14 along with other carbon atoms as part of their food. This Carbon 14 is then absorbed into their bodies. Scientists discovered that the speed with which these radioactive particles decay is always the same, so they could measure the amount of time that had passed since a living thing had died and stopped absorbing Carbon 14. For the first time ever, provided something had once been alive, it was possible to work out how old it was from this newly discovered radioactive clock.

It's impossible to exaggerate how important that discovery was to archaeology. At last there was such a thing as 'absolute' dating, a technique that didn't rely on

The basis of radio-carbon dating. Radioactive carbon (C14) is formed in the atmosphere by cosmic radiation and then absorbed by vegetation. This rots, is burnt, or is eaten by animals. All living things cease taking in Carbon 14 when they die. The Carbon 14 in wood, charcoal, bones, and so on decays at a constant rate that can be measured.

A slice of an ancient oak tree. The varying widths of the rings reflect the different factors affecting the tree's seasonal growth.

comparing what you'd found with something else, or hoping that it was from a particular age because it came from a particular level of archaeology.

Soon even more accurate dating techniques were developed. On Pueblo Indian sites in the USA scientists were measuring and comparing sequences of tree-rings in pinewood, which were giving them the felling dates of trees used in the construction of Indian buildings. This method, called dendrochronology, was developed for Northern Europe. Oaks were used as they have been the main construction material in much of the Northern Hemisphere for thousands of years. Nowadays it's possible to take samples of oak starting at the present day, back through timbers felled for eighteenth-century country houses, and beyond to those used in medieval church roofs and by the Romans. They can go further back too; right to the trees felled and worked by our prehistoric ancestors. From these samples we can create a complex chronology of rings of different widths which can be read on a computer and used to get felling dates for trees throughout Britain.

But it wasn't just wood that could now be dated. Countless different particles and processes were being measured, such as uranium, the spin of electrons, amino-acids, magnetism, heat and chlorine. All of these provided new dating techniques. Archaeologists no longer had to tear their long hair out trying to calculate dates. This left them free to investigate evidence on their sites that they'd never really looked at before. If Tutankhamun's tomb were to be opened for the first time today, archaeologists would be as interested in the information provided by the dust on the floor as they would be in the golden chariots. One golden chariot is pretty much like another, but the dust can tell you about the fortunes of a whole civilization.

This new archaeology has only just started to develop. Different ways of looking at the tiniest bits and pieces are constantly emerging. Take DNA analysis. It seems as though this technique will provide us with evidence about the lives and movements of early people that would have been unthinkable only a decade ago.

So a modern archaeological site isn't staffed just by diggers. There could be as many as twenty different specialists scrutinizing their chosen subject in minute detail and taking it away to research it. It's said that nowadays one week's digging will generate three months' work off site.

Samples of wood taken from a living tree, an eighteenth-century house, a medieval church roof and timbers from an excavation. The overlapping patterns of tree rings give the sequence which a newly excavated sample can be checked against for a date.

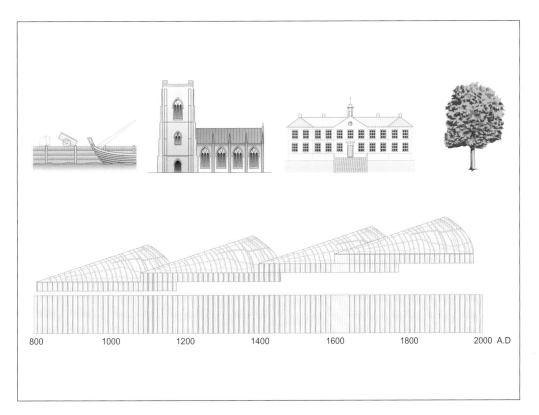

| 800 | 1000 | 1200 | 1400 | 1600 | 1800 | 2000 A.D |

Pollen grains.

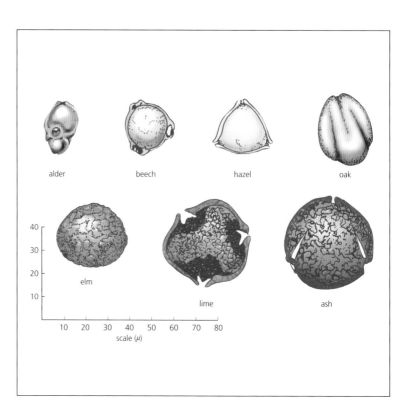

alder   beech   hazel   oak

40
30
20
10   elm

                    lime   ash

10 20 30 40 50 60 70 80
scale (μ)

Environmental archaeologists may turn up on site looking for evidence of ancient flora and fauna. Perishable materials like these don't always survive. Frozen or very dry conditions are good for preservation, but in Britain the best bet is to take samples from permanently waterlogged places. So they'll look for sodden materials like the damp stuff you took out of your pit. If they find burnt grain in it, they'll be able to learn about the types of crops grown, the foodstuffs eaten by the people who once lived there, and what sort of farming and processing techniques they used. Nuts, pips, seeds, twigs and bits of insects will tell them what the natural environment was like, what food was cultivated and what was available in the wild.

If there's a really big ditch, they may take a long vertical sample out of it. They'll deduce the types of vegetation that grew there, and how they changed over long periods of time. If the conditions are right, snails will occur – not the big fat ones that eat your lettuces, but tiny ones, often no bigger than a pinhead. These little gastropods are very fussy about where they live, some preferring damp, shady conditions, others liking dry, open grassland; so they're great indicators of different ancient environments.

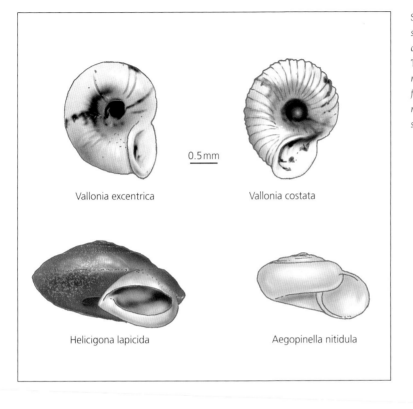

Vallonia excentrica

Vallonia costata

0.5 mm

Helicigona lapicida

Aegopinella nitidula

Small snails. The top two species indicate open conditions lacking woodland. The bottom left is found on rocks and in rubble foundations and the bottom right is found in damper shady conditions.

Bone specialists will identify the various domestic animals – pigs, sheep, oxen and the like. But they'll do more than that. They'll also look at the ratio of different animals, the age of the population of the different species, the butchers' marks on the bones and what all this tells us about the lives of the people who occupied the site. It's possible to work out, for example, whether a settlement was full of poor people eating rough, coarse-grained meat, or whether wealthy individuals lived there, stuffing themselves with fancy cuts like shoulder and hock. Or if 99 per cent of the bones in a pit are from sheep's feet, it's a reasonable guess that there was once a tanner close by, who kept the feet attached to the skins to provide a handle for stretching, then lopped them off after the process was completed.

Archaeo-metallurgists may come along too. When they find slag from metalworking, they'll put it under a microscope and examine its crystal structure to see how efficiently the iron has been extracted from the rock. From this they can work out what sort of technologies were available to the people who lived there, and what sort of artefacts they'd have been making. From an examination of stone items like quern-stones or axes, they can work out the

Preseli in Dyfed, Wales.
This impressive outcrop of
hard bluish stone was used
not only to make axes but
also for the smaller standing
stones at Stonehenge.

source of the rock from which the items were made. It was this process that proved the existence in Stone and Bronze Age Britain of a number of 'factories', rocky outcrops which were quarries from which stone axes were exported all over the country.

If there's a problem of dating on the site and a big timber is exposed, the dendrochronologists will be called in. They'll chain saw a block off the end of the wood or take a pencil-sized core out of it, and take it away for computer analysis. As long as some of the bark or the outer edge of the sapwood is intact, it should be possible to work out not only in which year, but in which season of that year, the tree was cut down.

Bone samples will be taken off for carbon dating. If there's a hearth or patch of burnt clay without a date, a scientist will be called in to work out how old it is from the magnetism in the clay.

Specialists such as these have totally transformed the way we look at our archaeology. In the 1900s archaeologists described their sites in a very dry way. They might have written that a particular site was Anglo Saxon with three phases of activity indicated by the types of coins and pottery in each stage. But today's archaeologists can bring that site to life, telling us that the landscape was

Dendrochronologist, Mick Worthington, at High Ercall in Shropshire, taking samples of oak from the roof of the manor house for tree-ring dating.

originally deciduous woodland, which was then cleared for grass and arable farming and finally degenerated into overgrown scrub. The people were sheep-farmers, but they also grew wheat, barley, peas and beans, and collected apples and sloes. The best quality meat was going to the rich people up the road, but an analysis of the finds tells us that the community was in contact with traders from Northern Germany, Cornwall and Turkey.

From top left, clockwise: A flotation unit in use. Water is continually recycled through the large containers while samples from pits, ditches and so on are put on to the mesh; This 'flot' can include carbonized seeds and grains (right) and other material such us pips, charcoal, snails and small bones – all of which can be used to build up a picture of the environment or economic life at a site; Professor Russel Coope and colleagues studying insect remains and small molluscs, 'Flot' samples from a site in Canterbury with pips and seeds clearly visible.

All this only forty or so years after the new technologies began to make their mark on British archaeology. Imagine how much more we may discover in the next forty!

Taking archaeomagnetic samples for dating at Canterbury from a well-preserved medieval tile kiln.

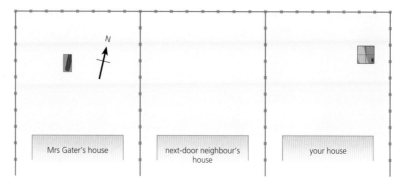

B ack at your house, you look over the fence into your next-door
neighbour's garden. Would he mind if you dug a trench there? You bet
he would. He's away at the moment on a three-month management
training course in Arbroath. But you're loath to sink even the smallest test-pit
into his lawn because he's a dull, humourless individual who's never shown
the slightest interest in anything cultural or historical. Fortunately there's Mrs
Gater. She's a very different kettle of fish. With luck you'll be able to talk her into
sacrificing a small corner of her unkempt vegetable patch for you to explore.

Armed with a box of chocolates and a neighbourly smile, you manage to
wheedle your way into her back garden. She couldn't be more helpful. She's
happy to let you dig wherever you want. Mind you, she's never shown much
interest in gardening. You have to move three rusty bikes, a cold frame, several
old radiators and an ancient central heating boiler before you can start.

On the basis of the work you've already done, you decide to dig a 2 x 1
metre trench. This should be big enough for you to work in, and hopefully will
show you if the archaeology in your garden extends this far. (You're now about 30
metres from Trench 1.)

You need to relate this new trench to the one in your garden. The best way to
do this is by measuring the distance on a large-scale Ordnance Survey map. But as

you haven't got one, and as your next-door neighbour's away, you clamber over the fence with a long tape measure and make the necessary measurements.

Then you repeat the excavation procedures you went through in your own garden and discover that there's certainly plenty of archaeology here, but there's one puzzling difference. The medieval layer you found in Trench 1 is completely absent. You've come straight down on to the yellowy 'Roman' level.

You begin to clean it up. Straight away you can see that along one side of this trench there's a darker mixed-up layer, still with lots of yellow material in it, but clearly different in colour and texture. Is it a ditch? Possibly not. It seems to be about 2 metres long with curves at both ends. You continue to clean in order to define its edges, but uncover something that at first glance appears to be a large sandy-coloured stone. More cleaning reveals it's larger than you'd first thought, with a line zig-zagging across it. When you tap it, it produces a hollow sound. It's not a stone at all! You can feel a sinking feeling

The trench in Mrs Gater's garden.

in your stomach. Is it what you're beginning to think it might be? It's the right colour. It's got those strange zig-zags on it. It's buried in something about the length of an adult human being. Have you uncovered a human skull? If so, what on earth do you do next?

Fortunately, at that moment, who should burst into your neighbour's garden but Frankie, the County Archaeologist (an amazing coincidence, but this is a work of fiction). She's about thirty-five, with bleached hair and a hoarse voice, and she's smoking a roll-up. In as calm a voice as you can manage, you tell her you think you've discovered a grave. Not only that but it looks like there's a Roman skeleton in it.

'Why do you think it's Roman?' she asks.

'Because it's in a Roman layer,' you reply.

She gives you a meaningful look then produces a trowel from the back pocket of her jeans, strides over to your trench, pulls off her black leather motorbike jacket and starts to clean the dark area you recently uncovered.

'Is it a grave?' you ask, trying to make it sound like a casual inquiry.

'Well, it's about 2 metres long, with a probable skull at one end. But you don't even know it's human yet.'

'Could it be modern?' you ask, glancing nervously towards the house. Then your voice drops to a conspiratorial whisper. 'Could it be a murder?'

Frankie explains that the fill's tightly packed, it hasn't got any air pockets and there's no topsoil mixed up in it so, murder or not, it's unlikely to be modern. After a bit more scraping she can see that the skull isn't from a pig or cow or any other animal likely to be buried here, but says the only way to be sure of what you've got is by digging it.

She shows you what to do. You start at the end where the skull is and take a centimetre of earth off all along the dark area. You work your way very carefully because if you come across any bones they may be very fragile. As you work your way down, you gradually reveal more of your curved piece of bone. First eye sockets, then a nose. It's definitely a skull, it's certainly human, and it's lying on its back.

But is this the only bone here or have you got the full skeleton? When you're about 3 centimetres further down more human remains appear. There are teeth, then a whole jaw.

Another centimetre and you discover bits of arm and pelvis and leg bone. It's exciting, but there's also part of you that's starting to feel a bit disappointed. You'd been hoping to find a skeleton like the ones medical students use in anatomy lessons, with all the bones in the shape of a human body and the jaw still working. Instead you've got a rather grubby pile of broken fragments. Because they've decayed, a lot of the bones are broken or eroded,

and some have simply disappeared. But Frankie warns you that you still have to be very careful as there may be finds close by. There could be parts of a coffin, or artefacts that were buried with the body.

What exactly where Romans buried with? Purses full of money? Weapons? You'll soon find out.

Then you discover something close by the right arm. You're pretty sure it's iron, but it's so lumpy and corroded you can't make out what it is. Frankie tells you it's a 'ferruginous mass', but as that means a lump of corroded iron you're not much the wiser. Part of it is long, thin and seems to narrow down to a point. Could it be a Roman spear?

Frankie thinks this is unlikely. Weapons are very rarely found in Roman graves. She thinks it's more likely to be Anglo-Saxon. You realize you'd made the mistake of assuming the bones were from the period of the layer you were excavating, forgetting that it was just as likely that they had been dug into that layer in a later period.

Excavation of an Anglo-Saxon grave at Winterbourne Gunner, Wiltshire. All that can be seen at this stage is the top of the skull (on the left). It's not yet clear if there will be any more of the skeleton in the grave.

An Anglo-Saxon skeleton in a grave at Raunds, Northamptonshire. Archaeologist Phil Harding is working with a dental pick. Note the soil sample in the plastic bag in the middle of the picture.

If it is an Anglo-Saxon skeleton there may be other finds. You could have a mass of fragile metal objects to disentangle.

It's then that you spot, dotted among the bones, two dull spherical objects. One's the size of a pea, the other's more like a marble. When you get really close you begin to think they may be glass. Are they coloured? It's hard to tell as they're covered in earth, but the small one appears to have a blue tinge, while the large one could be brown. Also, in the chest area of the body there's some green staining. Is there more metal close by? Another centimetre down you find it – a green corroded circular disc, about 4 centimetres across.

The skeleton in Mrs Gater's garden.

Frankie is now absolutely convinced the burial is Anglo-Saxon because of the nature of the finds. There's still an hour of daylight left. You're eager to start lifting the bones. But Frankie says it'll take a whole day and you need good light to do it. Anyway, she has to go back to the office now to scrutinize the assessment forms of the staff she manages.

'Honestly,' she says. 'That's the kind of cobblers we archaeologists have to do nowadays.'

You agree to wait until morning before you start lifting. If you'd been here on your own you'd have had to notify the police, but Frankie is happy to sort all that out and get the necessary Home Office licence.

Mrs Gater has just returned from Oddbins and you spend the evening with her poring over a book about Anglo-Saxon burials. You discover that, when they died, the Saxons were buried with their prized possessions and other valuable gifts. No one's sure whether this was to show how important the dead person was, or whether it was to equip them for their voyage into the next world. You try to work out what the mysterious rusty lump of metal might be. Is it one big object like an axe, or could it be a whole lot of things fused together in a great lump of corrosion like a pile of tools or a length of chain?

Later that night you fall asleep dreaming of your own voyage into the after-life, surrounded by your car-keys, Walkman, laptop and a small tin of extra-strong mints.

Next morning, bright and early, Frankie turns up at Mrs Gater's with a flask of tea, two fried egg sandwiches and two sealed plastic bags. You shake off your headache and mild nausea. You're ready to start work on the grave.

You clean right out to the sides of the grave cut, and all the way down to the bottom, so that the bones are completely exposed. It's a delicate and difficult job. You look at every spoonful of soil, checking for more beads or bits of metal. You even put the spoil in a special place, then work it through your garden sieve and run Colin's metal detector over it. It's worth the effort. You find a little encrusted metal object which you missed during the excavation.

Tony lying in his 'grave' with the possessions he would like to take into the next world, including his filofax, road atlas, bag, CDs, newspaper and mobile phone.

Your main problem is that you've only got a vague grasp of human anatomy. You've no idea how many bones a foot or a hand are supposed to have. And it's hard to tell the difference between the tiny bones and the surrounding pieces of gravel. Fortunately Frankie has got a somewhat scrumpled skeleton recording-form in one of her jacket pockets. It has a picture of a complete skeleton on it showing all the bones, so you can work out what to look for.

It's a long, slow day. Your trowel, which yesterday seemed such a delicate instrument, is too big and cumbersome to remove all the soil from round the bones. You have to use old dental picks, cocktail sticks and a small paintbrush. Frankie even has a handful of wooden lollipop sticks which won't scratch the bones.

It's important not to move any of them while you're cleaning. The position they're in will tell you a lot about the way the rite of burial was practised here. The Saxons had some very weird ways of burying their dead. Sometimes they laid them face down, while some were buried without their heads, or sometimes the head was put between their feet. Are the legs crossed? Are the hands at the side of the body or lying across the chest? Which direction is the body facing?

Soil being brushed from a skeleton prior to further excavation of a late Roman burial in a stone-lined grave at Ancaster, Lincolnshire.

SKELETON RECORDING SHEET

CONTEXT

SITE CODE	AREA/SECTION	TRENCH	TYPE
L: W:	GRAVE CUT	FILLS	COFFIN

SHADE BONES PRESENT AND MARK EXTENT OF TRUNCATION

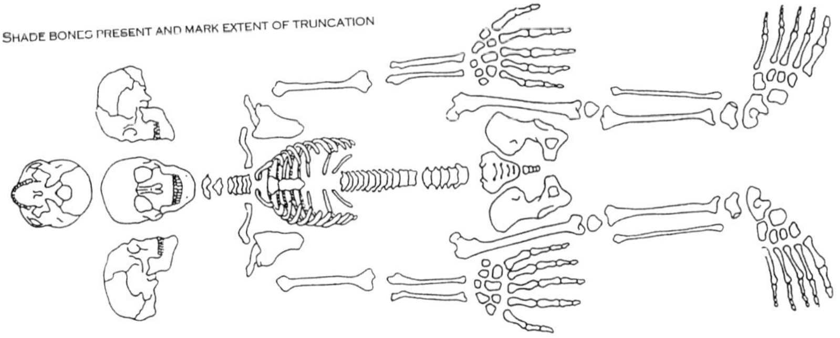

HEAD AT END OF GRAVE	CO-ORDS OF MARKERS 1	2	3	4
ATTITUDE OF:				
1. BODY				
2. HEAD				
3. RIGHT ARM, LOCATION OF RIGHT HAND				
4. LEFT ARM, LOCATION OF LEFT ARM				
5. RIGHT LEG				
6. LEFT LEG				
7. FEET				
8. EXTENT OF IN SITU BONE DEGENERATION				
9. STATE OF BONE AFTER LIFTING				
10. OTHER COMMENTS				
	INITIALS AND DATE			

ENVIRONMENTAL SAMPLES
No's

TYPE

LOCATION

DISCUSSION AND INTERPRETATION

FILL IN MATRIX AND LEVELS OVERLEAF

Eventually the cleaned-up bones and finds are standing proud at the bottom of the trench. It's time to record your work. By now one of Frankie's field officers has arrived. He's call Bodge, he has round glasses, hair down to his waist and a T-shirt with a big leaf on it. He's also got a camera and a 2-metre ranging rod, along with a number of little red and white painted wooden rulers which he lays in the grave to indicate the scale.

Next he gets out a little blackboard and a piece of chalk. He draws an arrow on the board to indicate where north is, and below it writes your neighbour's address. The skeleton has its own context number so he writes that on too. He places the board and the scale rulers beside the bones, then he snaps away. The orientation of the skeleton and its location will now go down to posterity.

He takes great pride in his photography. He makes sure the edges of the grave are crisply cut, that there are no traces of spoil left in the trench and that all the tools are cleared out of the way. When this trench is eventually filled back in, Bodge's photos will remain as a vivid visual record of what was

Photographing a newly cleaned section of a robbed-out medieval wall at Athelney, Somerset. Note the context number labels and the ranging rods (one metre in length).

Licence Number
File Number

LICENCE FOR THE REMOVAL OF HUMAN REMAINS

1. In virtue of the power vested in me by Section 25 of the Burial Act, 1857 (20 & 21 Vic., cap. 81), I hereby grant Licence for the removal of the remains of **persons unknown from the place in which they are now interred in the place known as**

2. It is a condition of this Licence that the following precautions shall be observed;

    a) The removal shall be effected with due care and attention to decency;

    b) The ground in which the remains are interred shall be screened from the public gaze while the work of removal is in progress;

    c) The remains shall, if of sufficient scientific interest, be examined by

    d) The remains shall, if of sufficient scientific interest, be retained for archival storage in   or they shall be re-interred in a burial ground in which interments may legally take place, and in any intervening period they shall be kept safely, privately and decently.

3. This Licence merely exempts from the penalties which would be incurred if the removal took place without a Licence; it does not in any way alter civil rights. It does not confer the right to bury the remains in any place where such right does not already exist.

4. This Licence expires on **24 May 2002**

David Blunkett

One of Her Majesty's Principal
Secretaries of State

HOME OFFICE
25 February 2002

Planning stone scatters and soil patches at Gear in Cornwall.

down here. Despite looking like an inner-city vagrant, he's a man of great pride and immense skill. He wants this dig to be remembered as an example of first-rate archaeology.

Now he produces a large metal object divided into 20-centimetre squares. It's a planning-frame used for drawing sites in detail. He lays it over the grave, and positions himself over it looking down on the skeleton. He's got a piece of gridded plastic tracing-paper which he's stuck on to a drawing board with masking tape. He transfers onto the tracing-paper the detail of what he can see in each grid of the frame. By the time he's finished, he's got an accurate scale-drawing of the skeleton and the whole trench.

When you embarked on this adventure you assumed the whole dig would take a few hours, after which you'd whip something of minor interest out of the ground. Three days later you're watching a hippy create a series of works of art and you still haven't lifted a single find from this trench.

At last, when he's finally finished recording, it's time to start lifting. Frankie produces a boxful of plastic bags for the bones and a collection of small plastic boxes packed with foam for the finds. You remove these first. Gingerly, each one is lifted from the soil beneath it and placed in a box with its own special finds label. Then the bones come up, beginning with the feet and gradually working up the body. They're put into boxes on acid-free tissue paper. Each foot and hand is placed in a separate bag, and marked 'left' or 'right'. When you get to the stomach, you take a sample of earth. A specialist may be able to get some clues from this sample about diet. As you work, the skeleton gradually disappears before your eyes, as the various limbs are bagged up and taken out of the trench. As you lift the pelvis, the tension mounts. Underneath it is another piece of iron, but it's impossible to work out what it is because it's so corroded.

Finally the skull is lifted. Bodge scrutinizes the earth one final time to make sure nothing's been missed and, after two hours, the grave's empty. You've been concentrating so hard that only Bodge has realized it's past opening time.

Over foaming pints of Adger's Skull Splitter – which Bodge assures you is the finest ale in the county – he tells you his life story. It's been ten years since he completed his archaeology degree. Since then he's worked all over the country. He's dug castles, deserted villages, Neolithic barrows, Iron Age settlements, post-medieval mansions, Tudor and Stuart gardens, seventeenth-century blast furnaces, a nineteenth-century watermill and a Bronze Age trackway. He's skilled, knowledgeable and dedicated, and he still lives in a caravan because he can't afford anywhere else. And his knees are dodgy, and his back's beginning to go. Archaeologists don't live very glamorous lives.

Next day you're in a room jam-packed with scientific equipment. It's full of microscopes and test-tubes, there's a big bench running down the middle piled high with archaeological finds, and its drawers are full to bursting with record sheets and computer print-outs. On the walls are a jumble of Health and Safety notices and torn posters of exotic archaeological sites in far-off places. There's a massive chart indicating who's working on what job. There are lots of dirty teacups, and piles of white coats hang from the doors. It looks like a cross between Frankenstein's laboratory and the store-room at the back of your local Argos.

This is the conservation lab. It's the regional centre for holding archaeological finds, and in your area it's attached to the local museum. You're standing next to

a large white humming X-ray machine, and the photos it's producing are bringing your grubby misshapen finds dramatically to life. You can now see that your two beads have got holes through the middle, and the smaller one appears to be a variety of shades of grey, which probably means it was made from different types of glass. What will it look like when it's cleaned up? It's too early to say yet.

The small metal object that you found in the loose spoil is a bronze pin. You can see that it's etched with little circles. The disc is in fact a brooch, with a circle of dots on it, and the metal object you found yesterday under the pelvis is a large knife with some sort of inlay set into it.

As for the mysterious 'ferruginous lump', the X-ray shows that it's made up of three different objects. One is the blade of a little knife, but the other two are still a puzzle. The smaller object is a strap-like piece of metal with curled-up ends, and the chunky bigger bit looks as if it's rectangular and about the size of a playing card. Over the other side of the room your bones are laid out on a table. For the first time they look like a proper skeleton, with all the bits in the right places. But there's something curious about them. The legs are thick and robust like a man's, but the fine features of the skull and the wide pelvic bones are more like a female's.

Inside the conservation lab at Salisbury. Time Team surveyor Carenza Lewis is looking at a bound-up Bronze Age cremation urn we excavated at Winterbourne Gunner.

Conservators cleaning a metal object.

Whatever sex the skeleton is, it clearly belonged to someone who had a healthy diet and didn't eat much sugar or starch. The skull has a fine set of teeth with virtually no sign of decay. But there's something odd about some of the bones. Their surface is rough and irregular and there are mysterious scratch-marks on them.

There's obviously plenty more information to be got here, but not yet. The lab's short of money and snowed under with work. Apart from the usual pot-repair work, metal-cleaning and typing up, this morning the local coroner demanded an urgent report on a hoard of silver coins that have been located near a local Roman villa site. You'll have to be patient.

You arrive back at Mrs Gater's. Now the high drama of removing the body is over, you've got more time to scrutinize the sides of the trench. You can see that the grave wasn't only cut through the yellow Roman layer, but also through a darker layer underneath it which lies directly on top of the natural gravel. You've no idea what this is, other than that it must be Roman or pre-Roman. What a wealth of material in two small trenches! There's Roman, Saxon and medieval in your garden, and Roman, Saxon and possibly something even earlier here at Mrs Gater's.

You shift your gaze to the back garden fence. Beyond it is a vast, scruffy, overgrown plot known as Norton's Field. Nobody's touched it for years. Imagine what fantastic archaeology might be lurking there!

Then you spot a brand-new brightly painted sign slap-bang in the middle of the field. It says: 'Coming soon to this site. A brand new Tesbury's development'. Your heart sinks. Tesbury's the supermarket people? Are they going to build some vast retail complex in Norton's Field? A massive hypermarket, complete with underground parking? If they are, acres of potential archaeological evidence could be completely trashed. You might have been able to prove that your skeleton lived in one of the very first Saxon settlements in the country. The Roman building could have been part of some huge palatial estate owned by the Emperor Hadrian. The medieval post-hole might have supported a huge silk canopy to keep the sun off the noble and elegant head of Queen Eleanor of Aquitaine. But whatever crucial evidence is in that field, it looks as though pretty soon it'll all be in a skip heading for the council dump.

Heinrich Schliemann, the excavator of Mycenae and Troy (1822-1890).

Well, maybe you were fantasizing a bit. Maybe it's unlikely you'll ever be able to prove there was a relationship between your post-hole and Queen Eleanor of Aquitaine. But is it possible to tie archaeology into the history of a period in that way? Could you ever pick up the base of a goblet with the absolute conviction that it once nestled in the podgy, bejewelled hand of Henry VIII?

At one time some archaeologists thought you could. Heinrich Schliemann was a nineteenth-century German banker, obsessed with the myth of the Trojan war. He was desperate to find the ancient city of Troy where, according to the blind poet Homer, Hector, Odysseus and Achilles were locked in battle over 3,000 years ago. In 1869 Schliemann discovered a little hill called Hissarlik in Turkey. He believed that underneath it was the city he was looking for. Unfortunately, in his desperation to justify his theory, he dug through layer after layer of archaeology until he found it. The site became famous. Mrs Schliemann's photograph was published in all the world's newspapers dressed in the jewellery they thought might once have adorned the fair face of Helen of Troy rather than the austere features of a German banker's wife (see page 102). But in fact Schliemann hadn't found Homer's Troy at all. Within three years of his death his theory was disproved by one of his co-workers. The jewellery and the site were authentic, but from a completely different period. Vast amounts of irreplaceable archaeology had been destroyed in the pursuit of a dream, and Hissarlik now looks like a bombsite. Some archaeologists say it's the worst case of deliberate archaeological vandalism they've ever seen. Good archaeology is about observing and recording what's actually there, not searching for something and then persuading yourself that the evidence fits your theory.

But even when archaeologists come up with cast-iron dating evidence, they can seldom do more than give us the general background of that period. They

can find settlements and field systems and create a picture of the environment, but archaeology is pretty useless at locating a particular moment of history in the ground.

Actually, that's not strictly true. Presumably the funeral of your Anglo-Saxon skeleton was a pretty big moment in the life of his or her family and it's been vividly recorded in the archaeology. But you don't know the name of the person whose skeleton you uncovered and you don't have a specific date for the burial. And in fact archaeologists seldom do.

Occasionally of course archaeology will coincide with a particular datable event. We know from contemporary records that Queen Boudicca burnt down the cities of Colchester, St Albans and London in AD 60. And there's a layer of burning in all three cities from around that time. Likewise, mass graves from the Black Death have been discovered in London and so can be dated to the

Hissarlik in Turkey. Schliemann's excavations while searching for the lost city of Troy.

catastrophic events of 1348. But usually, unless an archaeologist can find an actual inscription with a person's name and date on it in the right context, it's virtually impossible to prove a historical connection.

For instance, take the most famous event in English history, the one date we all remember: the Norman Conquest of 1066. It would have been a moment of gigantic significance for everyone involved in it, but would an archaeologist recognize it if he dug it up?

He'd certainly see profound changes in the archaeology of the period between AD 1050 and 1150. Massive castles appear all over the landscape in the macho new motte and bailey style. Thousands of churches and monasteries are rebuilt and renovated with entirely new layouts, and chunky, modern 'Norman' architecture replaces the simpler style used by the Saxons. There are subtler alterations too in the pottery styles and settlement patterns. But would our archaeologist be able to attribute all these changes to a seaborne invasion by a small group of heavily armed Frenchmen? And even if he could, would he be able to date these changes to the year 1066? It's pretty unlikely, isn't it?

So your theory that your medieval post-hole was part of Eleanor of Aquitaine's sun screen is highly unlikely ever to be proved. Never mind. Historically, there's still a lot you can tell from your trenches. Not surprisingly, you haven't come across any dates or named people, but you do have at least 2,000 years of human activity. You've got material from the Roman occupation (AD 43–410), and your coins and pottery should be able to give you a much more precise date within that timeframe.

You've also got evidence from the succeeding period (AD 410–1066), when Roman government broke down and the Saxons and other European groups invaded. This is the era we tend to call the Dark Ages because we know so little about what was going on then. In our ignorance, we tend to assume that life was dirty and fairly gruesome. This impression is reinforced by the fact that there's so little archaeology from that period and what there is can be pretty difficult to interpret. There are graves of course, and dark soil, dark rotting wood, dark pottery, and dark refuse pits. Maybe it isn't surprising our view of Anglo-Saxon times is so dark, even though lots of people were probably living the life of Riley. We certainly now know from the dig at Sutton Hoo in Suffolk and elsewhere that they had beautiful jewellery, magnificent helmets and incredible illuminated manuscripts. Compared with the later Normans, the Saxons were extremely sophisticated. Someone round here was certainly pretty well off. They dropped that beautiful coin of King Offa you found in your first trench.

You also have a medieval layer (AD 1066 to approximately 1500). This is a much more familiar period, populated by people we've all heard of like

Opposite: Madame Schliemann, wife of archaeologist Heinrich Schliemann, wearing ornaments found at Mycenae and supposed by her husband to be the property of Helen of Troy.

ANGLO-SAXON ARCHITECTURE

Saxon church at Escomb, Durham. The large windows and porch are later, but the small round-headed windows and large blocks at the quoins (corners) are characteristic of Saxon architecture.

Odda's chapel, Deerhurst, Gloucestershire. A plain late-Saxon chancel arch.

NORMAN ARCHITECTURE

Heath, Shropshire. A simple Norman church with round-headed doorway, typical of thousands of new churches built in the Norman period.

Kilpeck, Herefordshire. A more complex Norman church with a lot of carving and a very elaborate doorway.

Leonard Stanley, Gloucester-shire. A cross-shaped priory church with round-headed windows and doorways. In the foreground is the site of the cloister.

Much Wenlock, Shropshire. Elaborate overlapping round-headed Norman arcading in the monastery's chapter house.

William the Conqueror and Henry V. It's a time that's much easier to imagine because there's so much evidence of it still around us in parish churches, castles and manor houses. You've found pottery and bone indicating plenty of human activity, and your post-holes tell you there could once have been a medieval structure here – probably nothing to do with Queen Eleanor; more likely a peasant's house.

But you also know that at some time this building was abandoned, because there's a thick layer of soil on top of it full of post-medieval pottery. This isn't just unimportant earth. It's the next layer of archaeology – over 500 years of ploughing, manuring and grazing, which gradually built up until the moment when your house was built and the garden was laid out.

But this 2,000 years of activity isn't all you've discovered. Under the Roman layer in Mrs Gater's trench is a mysterious prehistoric layer. Not bad for a few days and two trenches.

Opposite: Exquisite artwork from the so-called Dark Ages. A page from the 'Lindisfarne Gospels'.

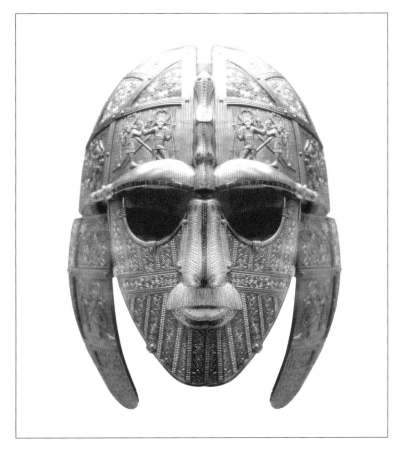

The seventh-century Saxon helmet from the Sutton Hoo site. Note the intricate decoration.

CHAPTER 9

The next couple of weeks are pretty frustrating. You want to keep digging until both back gardens look like a First World War battlefield. You even contemplate climbing over the fence in the dead of night and putting a little trench in the flowerbeds belonging to your neighbour in Arbroath. But Frankie is adamant that it's time to stop. This is partly for financial reasons. The finds you've produced so far have already tied up a lot of time at the conservation lab, and you've been using their facilities too, not to mention their budget. You don't want to overload them.

But more importantly you need to ask yourself what you'd gain by digging more holes. If you simply want to loot and plunder every possible find from every possible period then go ahead: turn your garden into an open-cast mine, and damn the consequences. But if your ambition has been to find out more about the history of the place, leave well alone. So far your excavation has been an exercise in key-hole surgery, what archaeologists call an evaluation or sampling strategy.

It's been tailor-made to answer the big questions that need to be asked about your site:

 Which periods are represented?

How big was the site in these different periods?

 What's the condition of the archaeology – has it for instance been trashed by ploughing or building?

You're already well on the way to answering all of the above. Excavation is destruction. You have to destroy what you find in order to understand it. If you carry on removing the irreplaceable evidence in your garden, it'll be useless to future generations. They'll have their own searching questions to ask of the archaeology and are likely to have infinitely more sophisticated techniques with which to interpret it. They won't thank you if there's nothing left for them to study.

This doesn't mean everything stops though. Lying on Frankie's desk is a file requesting outline planning permission for a supermarket in Norton's Field. You've mixed emotions about this. You like the idea of having to walk less than 20 metres to get your Shreddies and *OK* magazines, but you're not madly enthusiastic about a massive supermarket dominating your back garden. You're also puzzled. Why on earth was the planning application sent to an archaeologist?

This never used to be the case. Until fairly recently, a worryingly large amount of British archaeology was destroyed by foundation trenches, motorway construction, gravel pits and town centre development. But in the 1960s, more and more people began to realize how much of our heritage was being destroyed. The government began funding rescue archaeology in advance of big new construction sites, and local councils started employing archaeologists to tell them what archaeology there was in their area. Five hundred years after John Leland went stark staring mad trying to record the nation's monuments, County Sites and Monuments Records finally became a reality. But even though people in authority now knew where the important sites were, there was no law preventing developers trashing them in pursuit of profit.

In fact there still isn't. But in 1990 the government issued a document called PPG16, which transformed archaeology in England overnight. PPG stands for Planning Policy Guidance. It's not a law, but it means that before a planning application is agreed, local authorities can now require information about the potential archaeology on a site, in the same way that they'll want information about the ground water, the structural geology or any potential threat to the wildlife. So nowadays an archaeologist, acting on behalf of your local authority, will receive a copy of each planning application and, if necessary, ask the developer to get some evaluation trenches dug in order to find out what's down there.

This is the main reason why so many of Britain's archaeologists currently have a job. The digs they supervise are very different from the sort of research excavations undertaken every summer during the 1960s by universities and local archaeological societies. Often these went on for months or even years, and they tended to produce sack-loads of finds that were never properly analysed or written up.

Today archaeologists are usually much more meticulous when dealing with potential excavations. So how will Frankie treat the Tesbury's planning application? She wouldn't have had a great deal to go on without your work. Norton's Field isn't on the Sites and Monuments Record, there are no air photos showing potential archaeology, and there aren't any reported finds in the area. But because of the trenches you dug, she's convinced that this site could be of archaeological importance. She tells Tesbury's she wants a geophysical survey done and some evaluation trenches put in, and sends them a list of approved archaeological contractors. Tesbury's put out a tender and, after some furious undercutting, Westhampton Archaeology Trust gets the job. (Your site is over 200 miles from Westhampton, but archaeologists have to travel long distances nowadays in order to make a living.)

Anglo-Saxon pot found in a grave at Raunds, Northamptonshire.

Meanwhile you've had a message from the conservators. They've made a lot of progress with your finds and have invited you back for another look.

Your two beads have been transformed. You can now see that the smaller one is made up of blue and white swirling glass like a tiny blueberry and vanilla ice-cream, and the other is amber, prehistoric tree-resin from the Baltic, which is semi-transparent and honey-coloured. How this little Northern European bead got into Mrs Gater's garden we'll never know, but clearly there was some sort of trade going on here in Anglo-Saxon times.

The ironwork is still being cleaned. Removing the rust and corrosion is a long, time-consuming process. But the big news is that the puzzle of the ferruginous mass has finally been solved. The smaller strap-like piece is a fire-steel for making sparks for lighting fires and the bigger rectangular piece is a large buckle.

The knife found under the skeleton's pelvis has now been cleaned up and the corrosion blasted off with compressed air. The inlay is made of thin bits of silver sulphide called 'niello', which would have originally looked jet-black. The inlaid pieces appear to form a pattern, but it'll be some time before the conservators know for sure.

The bronze brooch has a detailed pattern of swirls, with traces of very fine gold-leaf on the surface. Originally it would have looked like solid gold. It's the Anglo-Saxon equivalent of today's costume jewellery. The conservator is particularly interested in the back of the brooch where there are clear signs of the weave of the cloth to which it was once pinned. Given how little we know about the Anglo-Saxon period, this is another good find. But how has this information survived? Doesn't cloth rot away within a few years of being buried? Usually it does, but not if the cloth's been poisoned as in this case. When the metal brooch began to break down, it leeched out its chemicals into the fibres of the cloth and killed off the micro-organisms that would have otherwise caused it to rot.

From tiny amounts of similar evidence throughout Europe, archaeologists have learnt a huge amount about Anglo-Saxon cloth-making, enough to know that your piece of cloth, which is pretty rare, is woven in the obscure '4 shed 2/2 broken diamond twill' style, and probably comes from the Syrian city of Palmyra. So you can now deduce not only that your Anglo-Saxon was buried fully clothed, but that he or she was wearing some rather fine imported clothes at the time.

Which brings you to the big question. What sex is the skeleton? At last the bones can tell you. Now the pelvis has been thoroughly cleaned it's clear she's female, even though her bones are so big. She was obviously a strapping wench. She wasn't a child – all her wisdom teeth have erupted. But the conservator can be much more precise about how old she was when she died, because there's one

Anglo-Saxon brooch from Winterbourne Gunner, Wiltshire.

superb age indicator. All her bones have stopped growing, with one exception. Her collar-bone hasn't yet fused to her breast-bone. This means that she was almost certainly over twenty-one years old but not yet thirty. She seems to have been in pretty good health. The only sign of physical infirmity is a healed broken upper arm, but that's so straight and well-healed that there must have been someone in her community with sufficient medical knowledge to set bones.

So why did such a strong, healthy woman die so young? When you were cleaning your trench you noticed some fragments that were so tiny and unprepossessing that you nearly ignored them. Then you realized they were bone splinters. Were they bird bones? You weren't sure, but you picked them up and bagged them anyway. It's now you begin to understand the value of collecting such small finds. These little bones are the remains of a tiny baby or unborn child. It looks as though complications in pregnancy or childbirth killed your Anglo-Saxon, a tragically common cause of death in Britain until the invention of modern medicine less than a hundred years ago. If you'd only removed the metal finds, this evidence would have been lost for ever.

But you now realize you made a big mistake. You failed to record the exact position of the bones before you picked them up. Had you done so, a specialist

Working out the sex of a skeleton. Note the wider hip bones in the female pelvis.

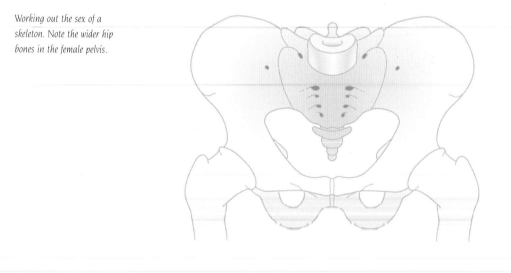

Male.

could have worked out if the child had died before, during or after birth. Because of your shoddy recording technique the full story will remain unknown. For the rest of the day you're much quieter than usual.

There's one final puzzle about your Anglo-Saxon woman that needs resolving: the strange marks and scratches on her leg bones. A bone specialist has looked at them and has come up with an answer. The marks were made by the teeth of a rat. But when were the poor woman's legs gnawed? Was it before she died? It's difficult to imagine how or why. Did she lie out in the open for some time after her death? Maybe the creature broke into her grave not long after she was buried. There are some riddles archaeology is unlikely to solve.

There's still plenty more that can be found out about her, though, but it'll require a great deal of analysis, much of which is very expensive. For now, her bones will be boxed up for storage.

You're not sure you like this idea. Some people argue that archaeological skeletons shouldn't be stored, and instead should be reburied. But if we're keen to learn about the people of the past, keeping their bones in a cardboard box in a museum may be preferable to burying them in a plastic bag in a

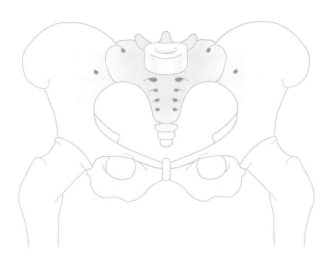

Female.

cemetery where they're likely to decompose within a year or so due to condensation and mould.

You're still not convinced. Isn't it treating someone with a lack of respect to sort through their bones, however long ago they died? Possibly. But maybe you're applying you own value judgements inappropriately. There are many periods of history in which people had a very different attitude from us towards death and the dead. At Eton, close to the college, a Bronze Age site has been found where the bones of the dead had been divided up, cut into pieces, processed, then dropped in a river. This certainly isn't the kind of behaviour we expect from today's public schoolboys, but may have been common practice in prehistoric times.

For the moment you're persuaded that, provided her remains are treated with respect, a cardboard box is probably the best place for your Anglo-Saxon woman. You'd certainly be reasonably happy for your bones to be dug up and examined by archaeologists after you'd been lying underground for 1,500 years.

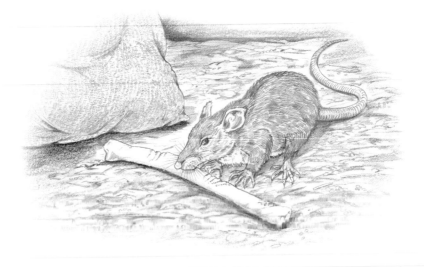

The conservator says she thinks it's important that there's a much wider debate on how bones are treated. It's an issue that's likely to generate a lot of upset and controversy in the future. As underground surveillance techniques become more sophisticated, greater numbers of skeletons will be uncovered, and there's bound to be a lot of publicity. Archaeologists' work is likely to be seriously affected unless the public are happy with the way the dead are treated.

For decades the archaeologists' dream was a machine that could see below ground. But before the 1980s, sub-surface surveying was such a cumbersome process that it was seldom used. Two things changed that – one was the development of lightweight equipment, and the other was PPG16, which stimulated a huge increase in the number of archaeological surveys and assessments.

The two geophysical techniques used most commonly are magnetometry and resistivity. A magnetometer has two sensors. One measures the Earth's magnetic field, the other the distortions in that field caused by features in the ground. By walking up and down a predetermined grid and logging the data with an on-board computer, plans of these variations can be plotted and any walls, ditches or burnt areas can be picked up.

Resistivity uses a machine like a zimmer frame with two prongs on the bottom. A weak electronic signal is sent through the soil from one prong to the other. If the current hits a wall or something similar that doesn't conduct electricity well, the machine will measure the resistance. On the other hand, if it passes through a ditch, or a pit or an area of waterlogged material, the current will flow quickly with no resistance, and that too can be measured.

It's impossible to stress how important these techniques have been for the archaeologist. In the past, if you didn't have any surface archaeology, your decision about where to start digging was often little more than inspired guesswork. But now, even if there's nothing at all showing above ground, trenches can be targeted with a degree of accuracy, speed and efficiency never before contemplated.

A spin-off from this has been that archaeology is now a much more attractive proposition for television companies. TV camera and sound crews no longer have to wait for weeks or months desperately hoping that something interesting will emerge from the ground. Three days will often provide sufficient material for a whole programme. This in turn has meant that more members of the general public have become interested in the subject, and demand for places on university archaeology courses is greater than ever before.

Above: *Magnetometer in use by Dr Chris Gaffney at Shapwick, Somerset.*

Top right: *John Gater carrying out a resistivity survey at Cirencester.*

Right: *Ground-penetrating radar at Athelney, Somerset.*

But before we get too carried away by the super-efficiency of 'geophys', it doesn't always work. Or at least it probably does, but we don't always understand the information it gives us.

A signal that seems to be an exciting prehistoric settlement may turn out to be a piece of magnetic rock or a layer of naturally deposited iron. Modern metalwork, power lines or buried cables can have an effect not just on the signals thrown up in the immediate vicinity but over a much wider area. Parked cars and portable radios – not to mention zips, watches, bra clips and nose rings – can distort the information. The seasons and weather conditions can cause problems.

You also need to have access to a big enough unobstructed area. If you try to survey a garden complete with fishponds and flowerbeds, a field full of high-growing crops, a forest or virtually any built-up area, you'll soon find your work seriously hampered.

Another drawback is that these geophysical techniques can't penetrate very far into the ground. Fortunately most British archaeology is within the top half-metre of the soil, but who knows what may be lurking deeper down, as yet unrecognized by geophys? One solution to this problem may be ground-penetrating radar. It's a potentially superb technique that's still in its infancy

but can already produce information from deep down in the form of jangly patterns of stripes. Unfortunately, as yet, there aren't many people who understand what they mean.

Chemical analysis is also one for the future. The countryside is full of clumps of nettles where a cottage or cowshed once stood. These clumps grow because nettles love phosphates, and animal and human manure are particularly rich in them. For years archaeologists have known that if they want to find settlements they should try digging near nettle patches, but phosphates aren't the only chemical elements that could be used to indicate where people have lived.

Gear in Cornwall, showing an Iron Age hill fort with internal round-houses and enclosures, overlaid by later field banks.

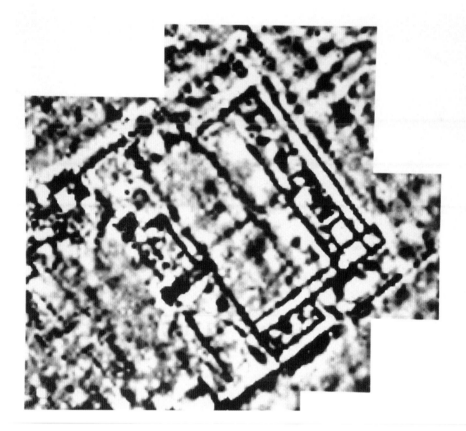

Turkdean in Gloucestershire: the geophysics showing the Roman villa with ranges of buildings around a central courtyard.

We now know that minute concentrations of lead, zinc, copper and manganese can be just as useful.

Clearly, a machine that could measure all these elements in their varying concentrations would be a phenomenal asset, and the extraordinary fact is that such a machine exists. It was developed by an American company and, since they're not using it any more, they'd probably be prepared to donate it to any archaeologist who wants to collect it. The only problem is it's on Mars, where it was sent to enable NASA scientists to look at the planet's surface geology.

Given the cost of developing such technology, very little work of this kind has yet been done on Earth. But as costs diminish, maybe in a few years' time we'll be able to do all our geophys and chemical analysis on a single machine towed along by a Land Rover or even controlled by a satellite. With this kind of technology, archaeologists could survey an apparently barren Neolithic site and learn where the pits and ditches were, where the people lived, where the

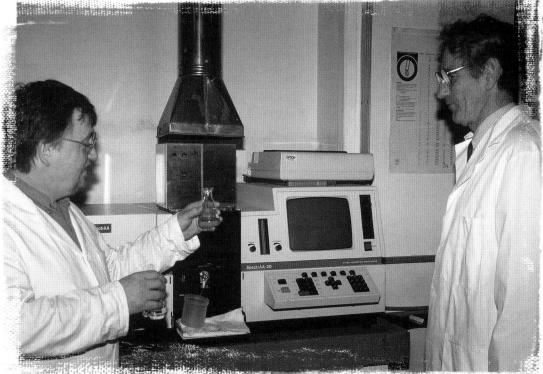

crops were grown and where the different kinds of domestic animals were kept. In other words, the whole pattern of life on a 5,000-year-old settlement site would be revealed before any digging took place, even though absolutely no structures still existed.

Unfortunately, you don't have the luxury of such advanced techniques on your site, but you are going to get a geophysical survey. You've been invited to a council of war. It's in the regional HQ of Tesbury's PLC, a big black glass building with palm trees and a small waterfall in the foyer. You step into a glass lift and are whizzed up to the very top floor while the fast bit from Vivaldi's Four Seasons plays softly from a hidden speaker. You're met by a young woman dressed in a black Armani suit, and wearing a touch of lipstick and small gold earrings. She takes you to the boardroom. It's got panoramic views across the town and a light blue sideboard with coffee, Danish pastries and fizzy water on it. You nibble an almond croissant and try to look relaxed, but you're a bit nervous. Under PPG16,

Preparing soil samples for heavy metal analysis at Bristol University.

developers have to pay for any archaeology that needs to be done. Will Tesbury's kick up rough? In the centre of the room is a round glass table. Sitting at it are a small, muscly woman called Sinead from Westhampton Archaeology Trust, who has a nose-stud and a sheaf of important-looking papers; a man in a suit who introduces himself as Philip Clarke, Tesbury's Strategy and New Developments Executive Officer; and an architect called Rod with a beard and a yellow bow-tie.

They're all listening intently to Frankie, who's telling them that from the work you've done she thinks there's a concentration of archaeology on your side of Norton's Field, from a number of different periods, but that it probably tapers off towards the far end of the site. Rod is clearly upset. He dramatically unfurls his plan for the new supermaret. There are towers, minarets, waterfalls, a lake, a huge car park and a large domed building. It looks like a cross between B&Q and the Taj Mahal and most of it's on your side of the field. Frankie explains that she wants a full geophysical survey and a number of evaluation trenches. She shows them on Rod's plan where the trenches should be located. One goes through the side of a large bell-tower, two through the Indian temple. There's an awkward pause, and a lot of dramatic sighing from Rod. Then the man from Tesbury's nods, says they'd better get on with it, and leaves the room. You're mightily relieved.

Processing geophysical data in the back of a jeep with a screen on which a plan of the results can be shown.

A few days later two harassed men in tracksuits arrive at Norton's Field in their jeep. They're ex-academics who run their own private geophysics company, and have been sub-contracted to do this job by Westhampton Archaeological Trust who are in charge of doing the excavation work. They immediately regale you with a long, involved story about problems they've had with their VAT inspector then, after a brief walk round the field, shake their heads gloomily and tell you what a difficult site this'll be to survey, and how full of inhibiting factors it is.

They lay out the field in 20-metre grids, then walk up and down each grid in turn recording the data. Periodically they download the information into a computer in the back of their 4 x 4, and after eight hours' dogged tramping half the field has been covered. You find the swirling colours and patterns of their printouts almost impossible to read, but even you can see the dramatic difference between what's going on in the area of the site closest to your garden, and the part furthest away towards the main road.

The geophysical survey of the Tesbury's site.

There are lines, or 'linear anomalies' as the geophysicists insist on calling them, which could be walls, and some of them are on the same alignment as the ones in your garden. There are lots of blotches and blobs that may well be pits or burnt areas. And there are other vaguely oval-shaped ones that are the same size and orientation as your Anglo-Saxon grave.

Meanwhile a rather earnest young man is putting shovelfuls of earth into plastic bags using the same grids as the geophys people. No one's quite sure who he's with or what he's doing. He identifies himself as Shahid, a student from the local university, and he explains that he wants to look at the soil chemistry to see whether the concentrates of heavy metals can tell him anything about the archaeology. Both Sinead and the geophysicists are sceptical about this, but he's not doing any harm, it's part of his research project and it might just lead to something, so they let him carry on.

You can't wait for the archaeology to begin, but Sinead says it already has. She explains that modern archaeology is about learning as much as you can from

*Taking soil samples for
analysis for heavy metals
at Shapwick, Somerset.
This site has been my pet
research project for the last
ten years – Mick.*

a site with the minimum number of holes and effort, so physics and chemistry are as important as the pick and the trowel. You nod thoughtfully as though you agree, but as you walk home you can feel your trowel itching in your back pocket. You really want to get digging again.

A few weeks later a small hut and a rather wobbly portaloo have miraculously appeared in Norton's Field. It's time for the evaluation to begin. A digger driver is waiting with a yellow mechanical digger, a copy of the *Sun*, several tattoos and a small sandy-coloured dog called Hendrix. Shortly afterwards Sinead and three other archaeologists turn up in a very old Ford Transit with a big painting of an Australian sunset on the side. They pore over the geophysics, do a lot of measuring and mark up the trenches that were agreed at the meeting with Tesbury's. They're going to dig a total of ten trenches covering 4 per cent of the field. Four of them will be dug over the oblong blobs that overlap the 'linears' coming out of your garden, while the other six will be sited further away on the side of the site which is pretty blank on the geophys. When you ask why so many trenches are to be sacrificed to a place where there's no archaeology, you're told that just because there isn't anything on the geophysics, it doesn't necessarily mean there won't be anything in the ground.

You offer the diggers coffee and custard creams, both of which are accepted with enthusiasm. Then the first trench is dug. The machine takes off the topsoil while Sinead, now sporting a light blue hard hat, watches closely to make sure the digger driver's toothless bucket doesn't go through any archaeology.

It's not long before they come down onto the subsoil. It's got bits of stone and dark patches in it like the stuff you saw in Context 2 in your garden.

Sinead sends the driver off to dig the next trench, while she and a couple of the others clean up the 30 x 2 metre slot he's left behind. The diggers let you work with them. You're impressed by the speed and accuracy with which they clean the trench, even though their trowels have been worn down to the size and shape of a teaspoon. Yours feels horribly large and new. You get the impression that, unlike other areas of life, the smaller the archaeologist's tool, the higher his status.

Your cleaning reveals the same kind of dark feature you uncovered in Mrs Gater's trench and which turned out to be an Anglo-Saxon grave, but in this case it's clearly associated with lines of stones similar to the Roman wall you discovered in the trench in your garden. This is the first time a clear relationship between these two features has cropped up. Previously you'd only seen them separated by the 15-metre width of the garden belonging to your next-door neighbour (who's no longer in Arbroath – he's been sent on a team-building course for middle executives in a forest near Abergavenny). If the dark feature is another Anglo-Saxon grave, it appears to have been cut through the wall of a Roman building. This is interesting in its own right, but it's also added confirmation that the wall is from an earlier period than Anglo-Saxon times.

One evaluation trench has got evidence of a wall in it like the one you found in your garden trench. Next to it are a few more tesserae, the same size as the ones in your garden but of different colours. This is the first and best indication that there might be a substantial piece of mosaic preserved somewhere in the field.

You ask what's happened to your medieval layer. Has it disappeared? You can't see it at all in this trench. Sinead doesn't know yet. Something odd is clearly happening between your garden and Norton's Field, but only a much larger excavation could sort it out, and there are no plans for such a dig at the moment.

By this time, the next trench has been dug. It seems to have another grave-cut in it, but the other end is full of gooey waterlogged material. The grave looks pretty exciting, but the gooey stuff seems fairly useless and slightly unpleasant.

Sinead doesn't agree. She thinks it's a lucky bonus. She doesn't know what it is, but it could provide some interesting work for the environmental specialists.

Over the next couple of weeks you keep digging. You learn more about archaeology, and about the archaeologists you're working with. They've all got degrees, some have two, one even has three! They start at 8 a.m. and finish at 5.30 p.m., and they're incredibly poorly paid.

Each lunchtime at one o'clock Sinead bellows, 'Clean up your loose!' This is followed by a couple of minutes scraping and sweeping, then one or two diggers disappear down to the pub for three-quarters of an hour. They eat prodigious amounts of food and you don't blame them. Sinead slightly disapproves of the fact that they drink at least a couple of pints of Adgers with their lunch, but in fact they're following a long historical tradition. Most Tudor and medieval labourers probably did the same – drinking alcohol was the safest way of consuming water in those days, and there's nothing like a drizzly afternoon in February digging through clay and mud to work off the booze!

Far too quickly the evaluation is over. The digger-driver, his yellow machine and Hendrix disappear, the archaeologists go off to prepare their report, and Norton's Field falls silent again.

Several weeks later you're back in Tesbury's boardroom. Rod is practically in tears. Frankie has just told him that the results of the evaluation show important archaeology and that, if Tesbury's insist on going ahead with his design as it's currently drawn, she'll recommend that the local council oppose it. She says she's quite happy for a supermarket to be built on the other end of the site where the evaluation trenches have shown it won't do any damage. But Rod is adamant.

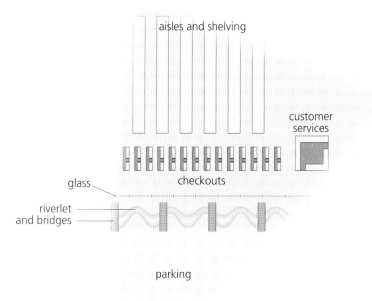

aisles and shelving

customer
services

glass

checkouts

riverlet
and bridges

parking

He says this would fundamentally compromise the artistic integrity of his
building. There's half an hour of passionate argument, with a lot of face-pulling
and pacing round the room. It looks like there's a complete stand-off. Everyone's
talking at once now except Philip Clarke. Gradually you all become aware that
the man who's going to make the decision hasn't said anything yet. The row
peters out. You all turn and look at him.

He starts by saying what a major aesthetic contribution to the town Rod's
building is going to be. He especially likes the twin spires, the clock tower and
the little hump-backed bridges which remind him of Venice by moonlight. In fact,
he says, he likes it so much that he would far rather re-site it on the far side of
the field than risk having to scrap it altogether. The car-park will be put at your
end of the field instead.

Part of Rod's plan for
the Tesbury's supermarket
in Norton's Field.

Frankie's more than happy with that. Any archaeology under the car-park will be preserved under a protective layer, and won't be wrecked by intrusive building. But she still wants an archaeological investigation of a substantial part of that bit of the site in order to understand what's down there.

Now the practical negotiations begin. How much archaeology will Tesbury's pay for? How big will the excavation be? How long a time-slot will the archaeologists be allowed before the builders move in? How much will it cost for Westhampton to keep a 'watching brief' over the rest of the site so that that any archaeology the builders turn up after the diggers have gone is properly recorded? By the time the meeting has finished, everyone's happy. Even Rod has cheered up because everyone agrees his building is a major leap forward in British retail architecture. He's even invited Frankie on an architectural day trip so he can show her his cutting-edge design work on the county's health centres and old people's homes. Unfortunately she's had to decline as she's currently snowed under drafting career evaluation assessments.

When the man from Tesbury's leaves the meeting, he's immediately surrounded by a small group of reporters. (They were actually tipped off by Frankie who has a monthly slot called D*ig This*! on the local radio station.) He announces that not only is he glad that local people will be getting such an exciting addition to their weekly shopping experience, but he's also very proud of the important work his company has generously funded Westhampton Archaeology Trust to do. It's a public relations triumph. Rod begins to wax lyrical about how his design combines Oriental, Renaissance-Italian and 1950s Californian influences in one ironic post-modern architectural statement. You decide it's time to leave.

Excavating early Stone Age remains at Elveden, Suffolk.
Notice that most of the archaeologists are wearing hard hats.

Time passes. Then one day the tranquil atmosphere of Norton's Field is broken again – this time by the sound of low-loaders. They buck up and down as they enter the site. Strapped onto one is a block of toilet facilities. On the other are two large portacabins. The little cabin and wobbly portaloo are taken away, which you feel quite sad about as you'd grown rather fond of that little loo. The new buildings are manhandled off the loaders and yanked into position. The portacabins are placed near the main gate where they'll function as an office and a lock-up for the tools. The new loos are located a little way off by a small clump of trees.

An hour later a battered minibus arrives and a dozen diggers clamber out. Several have brightly coloured hair, and there's the glint of ear, lip and nose rings. There's quite a lot of coughing as early morning roll-ups are lit, and much slurping of cheap instant coffee drunk out of chipped mugs.

*Site plan of evaluation
trenches (ET) and 50 x 50m
excavation in Norton's Field.*

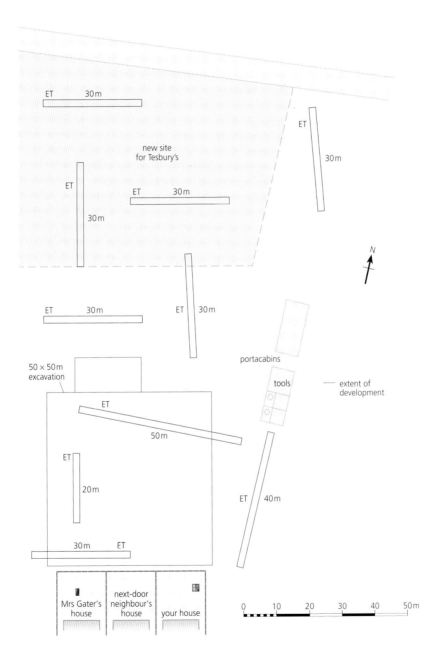

Sinead is the boss. Her assistant, the site-supervisor, is called Jock, presumably because he comes from Scotland. He's in charge of Health and Safety and jobs like laying out planks for the barrow runs and shoring up the deeper trenches.

They mark out the 50 x 50-metre site agreed with Tesbury's. Then it's time to start clearing the area. It looks as though there's plenty of topsoil over the archaeology, and this confirms what you discovered in your garden excavation. So Sinead decides it would be a waste of time to hand-dig it off. Instead the mechanical digger is brought back in, and the driver carefully takes off the top 30 centimetres. You're pleased to see Hendrix again, but he's not particularly enthusiastic about seeing you.

As soon as the first part of the site has been cleared, the archaeologists take over. Rows of hard hats bob up and down as the diggers scrape and clean. Jock's laying down some planks between the newly opened area and the spoil-heap. In fact he seems much happier doing this than actually digging. As the day progresses the spoil-heap gets higher and higher.

Gradually the site becomes more confusing. Soon it's a mass of different coloured patches. You thought the trench in your garden was complicated, but it now seems that this whole huge area is just as complex and it's a hundred times bigger. How on earth will anyone be able to work out what's going on, and which context is on top of which?

Hour after hour it's the same rhythm. Constant cleaning, the thud of picks and mattocks, earth flung into wheelbarrows, wheelbarrows creaking along barrow runs, earth tipped onto the spoil-heap. But this isn't the mindless removal of dirt from a hole. The archaeologists are continually asking themselves about the colour, texture and context of the material they're working with, then recording it and trying to understand what it all means.

There's a lot of thinking going on in the site hut too. As sections are cut and contexts removed, more information is discovered. New context sheets are being handed in all the time, providing a non-stop stream of evidence. Finds are scrutinized to try to pin down the dates of the different levels. The site-plan is constantly being reassessed.

There's one place that's particularly intriguing. It's a dark patch in a corner of the site where the geophys machine went haywire. Two archaeologists are dispatched to look at it, and you go along too. You're horrified when they attack the ground with mattocks rather than trowels. But they tell you that whatever the thing under here is, they're pretty sure it's modern, so they can use mattocks. It doesn't mean they aren't being careful. They have to treat it with some respect. It could be a tank of dumped chemicals, or even an unexploded bomb.

On the other hand, there's always the outside possibility that it's not modern at all. In fact, it might be something of real archaeological value like an ancient pottery kiln.

There's a ringing sound as a mattock hits something metal. A metre or so away another mattock comes down on something similar. Whatever it is, it's very big. What on earth could it be? Any minute now, you'll find out.

'Clear up your loose!' As soon as they hear Jock's cry, the archaeologists toddle off to lunch. You can't believe it. Have they no intellectual curiosity?

You tramp off with them to the site hut. Coffee's brewing. The same chipped mugs, adorned with a variety of advertisements and political slogans, are being passed around. The floor crackles with spilt sugar and discarded polystyrene cups. When you collapse into a threadbare armchair you realize you've sat on a soggy half-eaten packet of biscuits. The peeling Health and Safety notices on the walls look down disapprovingly.

Most of the diggers are vegetarian and eat what they consider to be a healthy balanced diet – hummus sandwiches, vegetarian pasties, crisps, Fanta and Mars bars. A few carnivores wolf down meat pies and chips. No one goes down the pub at lunchtime any more. That kind of thing is frowned on. But the local takeaway is going through a mini-boom.

Lunch lasts only half an hour. You tramp back to the mysterious object. It seems to be made of metal sheeting. The three of you hack through it into a void. After some trowel work at its edges you identify something made of chrome. You follow it along half a metre or so, and finally you're able to identify what it is. The roof trim of an old car. Slowly a Ford Anglia is revealed. Why the hell would anyone bury a Ford Anglia? This is another of archaeology's unsolved mysteries.

Sinead decides not to remove it. It's a problem she'll leave to Tesbury's.

By the end of Day 3 the site has become so confusing you've completely lost your archaeological bearings. But on Day 4 there's a ray of light. Down by your garden fence there's an area with a post-hole in it which looks remarkably like the ones you found in your garden trench. Further cleaning reveals more holes. It looks like you've found evidence of a rectangular building.

Then for the first time you realize why continual careful cleaning with the side of the trowel is so important. Initially, all the earth you're working on looks the same colour. But gradually it becomes clear that there are two different colours here. Outside the building the earth is darker, inside it's lighter. Then a third colour is revealed. It's a reddish texture in one corner of the building. What you've uncovered is evidence of a medieval peasant longhouse, in which the people lived at one end and the animals at the other. Yours is the inhabited end with its light clay floor and a hearth stained red from constant burning.

Why is a context called a context?

In the old days, if you found a post-hole, wall, pit, ditch, feature or layer on an archaeological site, that's what you called it. But there was often debate about the interpretation. After all, one person's layer is another person's feature.

So nowadays everything's given a unique number and for the purposes of recording is called a context. It's important to record each context and how it relates to other contexts as a series of events. For example, when you're describing the relationships between contexts, you need to show whether they overlie, underlie, cut, form the fill of, or are filled with other contexts. Each context represents a distinct event in the archaeological record. So a uniform layer of build-up that has taken place over a period of time represents one event and can be recorded as a single context. But the digging of a hole for a post is one context, the placing of the post in the hole another context, and the backfilling of the hole is a third (see diagram on page 58).

The interrelationships between these contexts can be represented in a matrix diagram (see opposite). Using this sort of diagram, a skilled archaeologist can see the relationship between the contexts found on the site and can relate them to adjacent trenches. This is a particularly useful system for sorting and ordering contexts on complex town sites when there are lots of complicated interrelated contexts.

What is a matrix diagram and what the hell is it for?

A matrix is a diagram that shows the interrelationships of contexts on a site. It's needed so that anyone else looking at the site records after the site has been dug away will be able to see what the excavator identified as the sequence of events when the site was being excavated.

It works by taking all the context sheets that have been filled in and sorting out their interrelationships – rather like a family tree. The top of the site is at the top of the diagram and you move on down through the excavation just as you do on site. So, in your garden Context 1 is the topsoil and, when you take this off, the next layer to be revealed is the medieval layer, Context 2. A post-hole has been cut into this layer, and is therefore later than the medieval Context 2. It has three context numbers (Contexts 3, 4 and 5 – see page 58) because they represent the three events of digging the hole (3), setting up the post (4) and packing the soil around it (5).

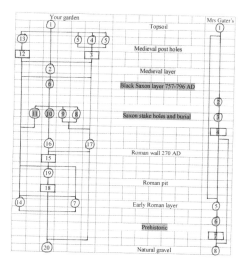

Mrs Gater's garden is a separate excavation so it has a separate set of context numbers. Starting once again with the topsoil as Context 1, you find that there's no medieval layer and her Context 5 is the orange Roman layer. Looking at the diagram you can see that this layer relates to Contexts 7 and 14 in your garden.

The other end, where the animals lived, is beyond the trench. There's lots of charcoal and animal bone outside the house and a wealth of broken bits of pottery. When all this rubbish is cleaned away, you discover two finds. The first is iron, and after the muck's been brushed off you realize it's a big key. Clearly security was a matter of importance in this peasant idyll!

The other is much more exotic. It's made of pewter (a mixture of lead and tin), and is a little picture of someone with a long, faintly ridiculous hat. It's a badge of St Thomas à Becket, which would have been owned by a pilgrim. Once upon a time someone around here must have gone on a pilgrimage on their 'holy days' to the saint's shrine at Canterbury.

Even more finds are coming up now. There's a piece of millstone and a badly corroded iron blade outside the building. Though your garden trench is just on the other side of the fence, the medieval post-holes there don't seem to belong to this building. This is exciting news. It could mean you've got at least two buildings, and two buildings could mean a medieval settlement.

The size of this medieval site is beginning to make sense too. You'd wondered why it didn't appear in Mrs Gater's garden and in much of the field. After having dug more extensively, it seems clear that medieval occupation took place in quite a small area. It can only be found in the south-east part of Norton's field and in your garden. Then it probably goes off further south-east under your house. It doesn't run as far as Mrs Gater's, so it probably peters out under the garden of your next-door neighbour (who's now left Abergavenny and is on a quality control assessment course in Scunthorpe).

Sinead did some background research before the dig started. Apparently documents say there was once a settlement round here called Norton. You're in Norton's Field, and 'ton' or 'tun' means farm. Could this be the site of the farming settlement that was originally known as North Ton?

Your musings are interrupted by the sound of engines. A fleet of minivans are arriving on site followed by a large crane. Then half a dozen portaloos appear. The builders are starting work on the supermarket. You're horrified. Have Tesbury's reneged on their agreement? Is the archaeology going to be trashed after all?

You phone the County Archaeology Unit in a rage. You want to go down to Tesbury's and have it out with that Philip Clarke immediately. Frankie says relax, don't do it. The geophys and evaluation trenches have shown that there isn't any significant archaeology on the far side of the site, and because a good relationship has been developed with Tesbury's, there's no reason why building work shouldn't begin there straight away, even though the archaeologists are still on site. Actually it's a positive advantage to both sides if everyone's working at the same time. Tesbury's will benefit because they can start building sooner, and the archaeology will benefit because, when the foundations and pipe-trenches are being laid, the diggers will be around. So if anything unexpected turns up, they'll be able to deal with it there and then.

Sinead needs someone to liaise with the builders, and everyone thinks a young, fit-looking digger called Katie-Jane would be perfect for the job. From now on she'll pop over to the building site three or four times a day to check whether any archaeology is coming to light, and it's generally agreed that the builders will be particularly happy to come to her if they spot anything that looks vaguely ancient.

Relieved, you go back to excavating your medieval trench. Soon there's nothing left of North Ton except two post-holes. All the rest has been scraped, trowelled and dug away. Archaeology isn't just rubbish, remember: it's also destruction.

Next day the archaeologists turn their attention to the oval shapes that look like the grave-cut at Mrs Gater's. Sinead is confident there's an Anglo-Saxon cemetery here. The diggers start the slow, concentrated work of exposing the skeletons. The first one they lift isn't in nearly such good condition as the one at Mrs Gater's. Its legs and half the head have been sliced off by medieval ploughing, but there are a couple of Anglo-Saxon beads with it, so it can be dated pretty confidently.

The diggers' work is temporarily halted when the press turn up and want a photograph. They've been invited by Frankie, who's trying to give the County

Washing Roman finds from an excavation at Cirencester with old toothbrushes!

Archaeology Unit a higher profile because she's nervous her funds will be cut next year. The photographers are concentrating so hard on getting good pictures that they keep treading on the edges of the trenches, dislodging little avalanches of earth which tumble down onto the archaeology. They put the diggers in unnatural poses round the skeleton, and for one photo you're reluctantly persuaded to join them. Then the reporters ask a few questions but don't seem to listen to the answers. Fifteen minutes later they've all gone again.

Soon the first week of excavation is over. And what a great week it's been! You've got at least six Anglo-Saxon burials, a newly discovered medieval settlement and goodness only knows what was going on here in Roman times! In addition, over in the corner of the excavation, there's a dark, wet grubby area unlike anything else you've seen so far. What on earth could it be? It's going to be a very frustrating weekend waiting for the action to begin again.

That evening, you sit down with the local paper. There, staring back at you, is your own face. It's the photo of you squatting by the Anglo-Saxon grave, grinning nervously. You're about to cut it out to send to your aunt in Bury St Edmunds when you notice they've spelt your name wrong and put ten years on your age. This misinformation is compounded when you turn on the TV and the

local reporter tells you that in Norton's Field there's the first Roman villa ever discovered in the county. Given that no one's sure the building is Roman, let alone whether or not it's a villa, it's hard to believe it's your site the reporter's talking about. Still, it's good publicity for the County Archaeology Unit, and at least he describes the Anglo-Saxon graves reasonably accurately.

Next day, Saturday, you look moodily out of your bedroom window at what you expect to be a completely empty Norton's Field. But it's far from empty. There are at least thirty adults milling around, the portacabins are open, and a dozen children are running about between the trenches.

You pull your clothes on and hot-foot it over to the site. Sinead should be having the weekend off. Instead, she'd invited the town's archaeology society and the local Young Archaeologists' Club to have a look round. But this isn't just a site-seeing tour. They're here to work. There are about twenty trays of finds that the archaeologists haven't had time to clean yet, and even the ones that are clean need labelling. The more experienced volunteers are given the job of writing the labels, while those who don't really know what they're doing are handed washing-up bowls and toothbrushes, and set to work scrubbing pieces of pot.

Marking finds. Once the finds are dried, in this case on old egg trays, they are marked with indelible Indian ink with a code showing where they were found.

For the best part of four hours they beaver away up to their elbows in mud and cold water. It doesn't seem a particularly fun way to spend a Saturday morning, but they all look happy enough, particularly when Sinead gives them a long and graphic tour of the trenches. But soon they've gone and you're on your own again.

The rest of Saturday and Sunday go by achingly slowly. What's in those Anglo-Saxon graves? Are you going to discover a Roman mosaic? You'll just have to wait until Monday morning to find out.

Eventually the new week begins. You arrive on site full of excitement, but there's a police car parked in front of the portacabins, and two policemen are talking to Sinead, who's clearly very upset about something. The diggers are sitting in small groups, not saying much. One of them is crying. At first you think there's been an accident, then you look at the site and your heart sinks. Some time over the weekend someone's broken in and robbed one of the Anglo-Saxon graves.

Ancient artefacts, especially if they're made of silver or gold, have always been seen as a good way of making money. As far back as the time of the Pharaohs, tombs have been looted and archaeological sites ransacked. But over the last hundred years or so many more people have realized how important our heritage is. Popular interest in the past is greater than ever before.

As a result, dealing in ancient artefacts has become a huge international business. Some are now worth a fortune, and are as good a financial investment as classical paintings or gold bars. This trade isn't new – many pieces have spent centuries being bought and sold by one collector or museum after another. But with so many people wanting a slice of the action, the supply of legal antiquities hasn't been able to keep up. The result has been an astronomical rise in the desecration of ancient monuments and illegal digging on archaeological sites.

This is especially true of finds you could define as 'art'. In Cyprus, thieves rip mosaics off the walls of churches. In Peru, the graves of Incas are bulldozed for pots, gold and preserved textiles. In Africa, poor villagers sell their heritage to unscrupulous art dealers. Sometimes museums are so keen to improve their collections that they buy artefacts on the antiquities market without asking any awkward questions. This has happened all over the world, and has involved some of the most internationally famous museums.

And it's not just museums and international investors that take part in this trade. There are tens of thousands of private collectors willing to buy Roman coins and pottery, Stone Age axes, Bronze Age tools and Saxon brooches, which they know have been found illegally.

But archaeological finds aren't just valuable or useful information in their own right. It's where they're from that matters – and that's called 'provenance'. Provenance helps us understand what things were made where, what techniques were available and how they developed, how the artefacts were traded and so on. Often, though, when an antiquity appears on the market, either the provenance has been lost or a fake provenance is claimed, in order to make it worth more.

In Britain most finds of any value are supposed to be subjected to a legal process, but there are unscrupulous finders who fail to report them and sell them on the open market, often with a false provenance so the guilty parties can't be traced. Most people would regard this as the theft of our heritage. Surely such finds belong to the nation? They ought to be on display in a museum, or at least be properly recorded before disposal on the market.

The issue may seem black and white, but what should be done about ordinary people with no criminal intent who pick up things in fields and take them home? What about the 30,000-strong army of metal detectorists who every weekend, criss-cross the British countryside in pursuit of metal objects? Should

Plundering Pharaoh: Theban tomb-robbers at work.

Bent coins

Coin hoards are supposed to be declared in Britain. They go through a legal process, they get subjected to analysis and recording, and there's an opportunity for professional archaeologists to examine the site as quickly as possible to recover evidence about the context. Then a coroner makes a decision on whether the hoard should go to the Crown with the finder and landowner getting compensation, or whether it should be returned to the finder. At that point, it's quite normal and legal for the hoard of coins to be sold on the open market.

But sometimes the finders never declare their discovery. Hoards of Roman coins, which have never been reported, are advertised on the internet, and bought by collectors or businessmen on the other side of the world who keep their purchases locked away where no one can see them or study the information they have to give us.

they be allowed to keep them without putting the information on public record? Should they be allowed to keep them at all?

After all, archaeology is as much a part of the environment as our birds' eggs, our orchids, and our village ponds. It's generally accepted that these are too valuable to be treated as personal trophies, but what about Roman brooches? If each one of those 30,000 metal detectorists picks up twenty metal objects a year and they're not recorded, over half a million irreplaceable artefacts are lost to us, not to mention all the valuable knowledge we could draw from them if they were found in context.

Except it's not as simple as that. For a start, many of those objects are in the plough-soil and long since removed from their original contexts. In fact, modern ploughing techniques are doing far more damage to Britain's archaeology than all the thieves, predators and humble metal detectorists put together. Not only that, it's sometimes the collectors who do the donkey-work. To this day, museums across the country depend on books about Iron Age, Roman and Saxon finds that are written and illustrated by collectors. Indeed, some of the most important finds from Roman Britain are detector finds. The Thetford Treasure was missed by the archaeologists. If it hadn't been recovered by a detectorist, thirty-three silver spoons and twenty-two gold rings, not to mention gold bracelets, chains and buckles, would now be concreted into the foundations of a factory. And every day on archaeological sites all over Britain metal detectorists discover metal artefacts and finds so small they would otherwise end up on the spoil-heap.

So should metal detecting be licensed, banned or encouraged? In the 1990s archaeologists decided that the way forward was co-operation. That way, the information haemorrhaging out through unreported finds and illegal digging could be slowed down, if not stopped. The result was the Portable Antiquities Scheme, funded by the National Lottery. Portable Antiquities Officers visit metal detectorists and their metal-detecting clubs to encourage them to record their finds and the specific circumstances in which they were found.

Unfortunately, the scheme's only a voluntary one. Many detectorists are happy to work with archaeologists, but others want to continue on their own, holding on to their finds without reporting them. The scheme is further undermined by the fact that there's no money available to help fund the conservation, analysis and study of the finds once they've been handed in, so every new find presents a potential financial problem. There's no doubt that the scheme's very useful, and detectorists are contributing a great deal more to archaeology by being part of it. But on its own, it's not a solution to the erosion of British archaeology that's continually taking place.

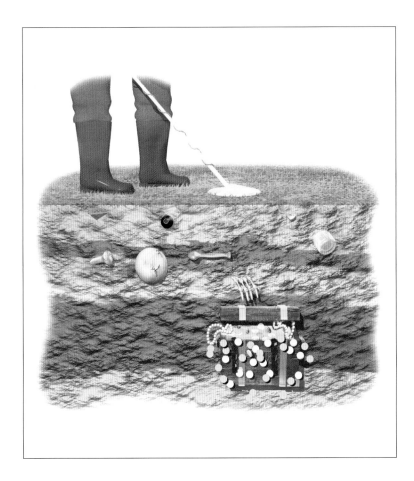

There are other problems too. Many people dream of finding buried treasure. In England and Wales, if archaeological finds are declared to be 'Treasure' that means the Crown can keep them, and the finder and landowner are compensated at market value. But is that the right way to use taxpayers' money? And suppose the British Museum decides it doesn't want to purchase them, and your local museum is given the opportunity to raise the money to buy them. Should small under-funded museums have to grub around to get the cash together to obtain important finds? Many museums are being snowed under, and some virtually bankrupted, by hoards of objects that have been designated as 'Treasure' so must now be purchased, conserved, analysed and studied.

Perhaps museums shouldn't buy these finds. But if they didn't, it would encourage finders to sell their discoveries on the open market. It's a tricky problem.

Even when valuable objects are given to museums for free they can cause a problem. Without the context they're found in, they're of virtually no archaeological value. That coin of Gordian you found in your trench isn't important just because it's old, rare, or looks nice. It's valuable because it can tell you about the archaeology in your garden. If a hundred coins like it were handed over to your local museum along with an assortment of belt buckles, scabbard ends, strap ends and brooches, all without a detailed context or provenance, they wouldn't be

Archaeologists with dirty hands

It's up to archaeologists to set an example. Most of them will go to any lengths to record their work fully and then publish it. But the sad truth is that this hasn't always been done, even on some of the most important sites in Britain. Sometimes twenty or thirty years go by and there's still no full report. Even worse, sites have been excavated by professional archaeologists and the records and notes and even the finds have been lost.

Why does this happen? There are many reasons. It can be because of a shortage of funds, professional jealousy, or just plain old incompetence. Today, even the change in computer formats is creating problems. In the 1980s digs were often recorded in formats that no present-day computer can read. It's difficult for archaeology to point the finger of blame at others when its own house isn't yet completely in order.

What is treasure?

The 1996 Treasure Act defines Treasure as:

1   Any object over 300 years old, except a coin, that's at least 10 per cent gold or silver.

2   All coins from the same find so long as they're over 300 years old, and that there are at least two coins which are 10 per cent or more silver or gold, or at least ten coins which are less than 10 per cent silver or gold, or made of base metal.

3   Any object associated with the Treasure, regardless of what it's made of.

By law a finder should inform the coroner within fourteen days of discovery.

archaeology. They'd be a historical mish-mash lying around wasting storage space and gathering dust. It'd be like sneaking a handful of rare bird's eggs from under their unsuspecting mother, presenting them to the people at the RSPB and telling them you'd forgotten where the nest was.

There's little doubt that a long-term national and international strategy needs to be put in place to sort out who should own what, to establish whether new laws are needed to protect archaeological finds and sites and to work out where the money should come from to ensure that we're all able to share in the world's archaeological heritage.

But the first priority is to make everyone aware of the amount of organized theft of archaeology that goes on right under our noses. There are gangs who set out deliberately to loot sites where they know the pickings will be rich. They operate at night, and cynically destroy whatever they're not interested in just to get their hands on artefacts they can sell. Thieves like these are seldom caught and when they are, the sentences are usually absurdly lenient. Such people are sometimes sensationalized by the tabloid press as 'night-hawks'. It was a gang like this that visited Norton's Field last night.

You look at the shattered remains of the grave you discovered just three days ago. The thieves must have heard about it on TV, then broken in when they knew no one was around. These weren't amateurs or young tearaways. They cut the padlock on the front gate with bolt cutters and had enough archaeological knowledge to know that an Anglo-Saxon skeleton might be buried with valuable finds and, presumably they knew someone who'd buy the finds off them.

They've dug up the grave as thoroughly as if they'd been digging for potatoes. There are broken bones everywhere. The grave-cut and all the contents have been wrecked. The skull's been hit with a shovel and has caved in. The archaeologists are gently picking through the debris, but they doubt if there'll be any finds left. A policeman says it's unlikely they'll ever find the culprits, but it hardly needed to be said.

The archaeologists aren't only upset, they're deeply frustrated. They'll have to put all their other work on hold in order to lift the rest of the skeletons as quickly as possible. Someone says there's so much theft nowadays that maybe they should always remove the valuable finds from a site straight away even if it means compromising other archaeological work. They phone a local metal detectorist who often works with the unit, and he says he'll come straight over and check the rest of the graves for metal objects.

The unit divides into four teams, and you begin to excavate. All thoughts of tea-breaks, lunch break and a 5.30 pm finish have long evaporated. You've got to work coolly and methodically, but it's vital that you get all the bones lifted before the light goes. There's no gossiping or banter today. You work in virtual silence.

By lunchtime you've cleared the earth round your skeleton. From the look of the hip-bones and the shape of the head it's probably a female. You've also got what appears to be an amber bead, but it's not as big as the one you found before. Initially you're disappointed. It seems as though this skeleton isn't going to be as interesting as your first one. But then you find another bead, then a third, and they appear to be in good condition. Soon you've got a dozen tiny beads, and close by, resting on your skeleton's collar bones, two saucer shaped brooches. These would have fastened her clothes. Maybe the beads ran in a string across her chest from one brooch to the other.

The female skeleton with brooches and other finds, in Norton's Field.

brooches

beads

comb

knife

girdle
hanger

Anglo-Saxon girdle hanger.

Anglo-Saxon antler comb.

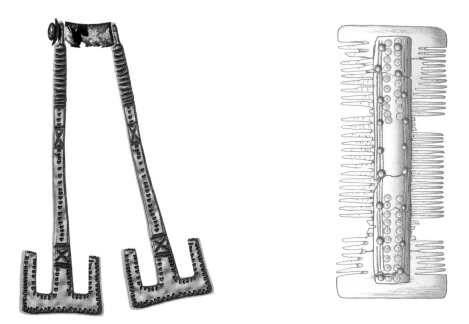

Near her waist is a knife. It's pretty big, the kind of thing she'd have used for household tasks and for cutting up her food. She'd also have eaten off it – forks weren't invented for another thousand years. There's no handle, because it would have been made of something perishable like wood or horn, but it would probably have been quite elaborate. The most fascinating find, though, is a flat T-shaped piece of bronze, about 12 centimetres long and decorated with stamped crescents. It's a bit like a Roman key, but doesn't look as though it could have actually worked in a lock. What's it for then? It's part of a girdle-hanger. In the idyllic world of the early Anglo-Saxons no one seems to have locked their doors, so no keys were needed. But there was still status in having possessions or a house which in more unlawful times might have needed to be locked. So women in authority displayed these girdle-hangers on their belts as symbols of the fact that they were in control of security. This lasted only until the end of the seventh century. Then, with the coming of powerful kings and priests, all that changed – real keys and padlocks re-emerged, and have been with us ever since.

Double burial with bucket, shield boss, brooch and other objects at Breamore, Hampshire.

So who was this woman? The girdle-hanger certainly indicates that she was a person of high status. Maybe she was responsible for a large house. Perhaps she was the most senior woman in the household in charge of security, valuables and the like. After the events of last night, you're surprised she hasn't turned in her grave.

When the bones are lifted you discover a large rectangular antler comb underneath her. The teeth are well preserved. They're thick on one side of the comb but thin on the other. You assume this is a nit comb, but in fact it's another highly prized status symbol. To be buried with something as valuable as this confirms that she was a power in the community.

Two of the other graves are in fairly poor condition. The medieval ploughmen have taken lumps out of them and the only finds are a couple of pieces of corroded metal that look pretty much like the knife you found at Mrs Gater's. But the fourth grave is a beauty. In order to dig it, the original Anglo-Saxon grave-digger hacked right through the wall of a Roman building. Why did he bother? Why didn't he just dig in softer ground elsewhere?

The final grave-cut is big and deep, and in the bottom is the skeleton of a young adult male. The bones indicate that when he died he was fit and in the

Burial of an Anglo-Saxon woman with saucer brooch and bead at Winterbourne Gunner, Wiltshire.

prime of life. There's what looks like a spearhead by his shoulder and something you instantly recognize as a ferruginous lump on his ribs. Could it be a shield boss? There's also a long piece of metal by his leg-bone. It's got Sinead highly excited. It's very corroded, but she thinks it's his sword! One this big would have been a very high status symbol – a bit like being buried with your new Mercedes. An X-ray, followed by weeks of conservation, could transform this cruddy piece

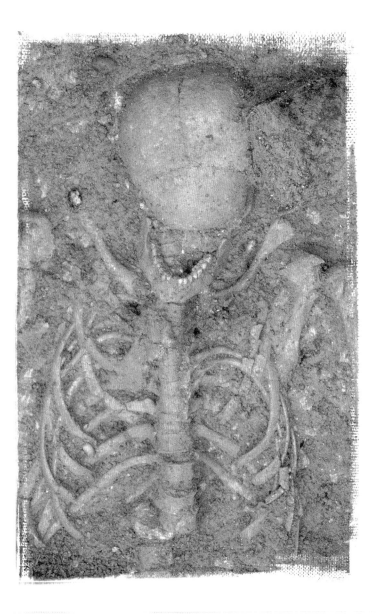

Burial of Anglo-Saxon woman at Raunds, Northamptonshire. Next to the head is an Anglo-Saxon pot, and a brooch.

The warrior skeleton from
Norton's Field.

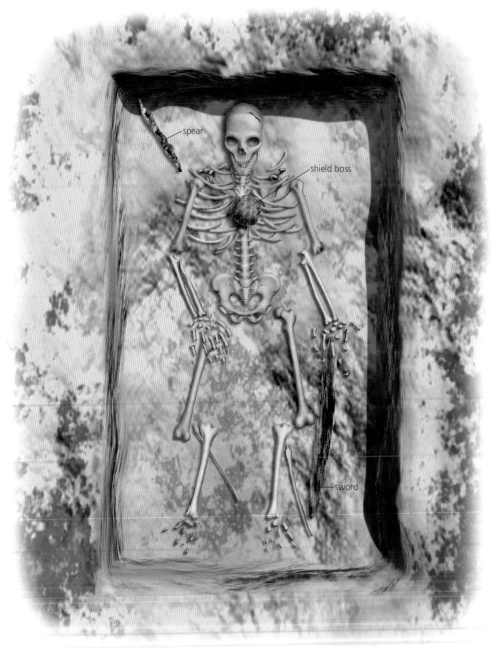

Mystery cemeteries

No one really knows why the Anglo-Saxons often buried their dead in places where their Roman predecessors once lived. It can't have been because such sites were particularly attractive. They'd often been abandoned for centuries, and must have been little more than piles of rubble. Maybe it was because the Anglo-Saxons knew that people had lived there before in the dim and distant past. Maybe they wanted to show that they too had a right to be on this land, so got themselves buried in the same place. On the other hand, maybe they just thought it was more practical to bury someone in a pile of rubble than in the good farmland surrounding it!

of metal into an amazing find. It may be pattern-welded: different pieces of steel and iron hammered together to create a strong, flexible weapon. It might be inlaid. It may have runes on it spelling out the sword's name – that's not so far-fetched. At this time swords were given their own character, just as some sad people nowadays name their Fiat Bravos, and even sadder ones have personalized number plates.

But however significant the sword might be, the most dramatic find is the state of the warrior's skull. It's got what appears to be a great gash in it. Whether this is the result of recent damage by the mechanical digger or whether it's an ancient, possibly fatal wound, only an osteo-archaeologist will be able to say.

There's one other mystery Frankie would like to sort out. A number of the skulls are strikingly similar. Could this be a family group? She wants to test their DNA, so she collects a healthy tooth from each skeleton. (She chooses lower canines if they've survived because they've got a simple structure.) The DNA specialist will drill through each tooth and test the uncontaminated dental pulp, but this is an expensive process and it'll be some time before you get any answers.

Beauport Park, Sussex.
The corner of a room in a
Roman building with the
flue tiles set in the wall.

Later, as the last glimmer of daylight fades, the final bones are bagged and the skeletons and finds are boxed up and driven to the museum. Even the remnants of the smashed up skeleton have been collected, although it's doubtful they'll have much of a story to tell. You're happy that the work's all done, but you can't help wondering what that skeleton could have told you if it had been left intact. You're starting to get a vivid picture of this Anglo-Saxon community, but it will never be complete because of the theft. Information has been lost for ever, in exchange for a quick and easy profit. Still, the site's now no longer attractive to greedy humans; hopefully the only predators tonight will be cats and owls.

Slowly the memory of that horrible day begins to fade, and work gets back to normal. The following week is spent looking at the Roman part of the excavation. The geophys results gave the impression that you'd find the remains of walls across the middle of the site surrounded by rubble. The excavation confirms this. You seem to have two rooms on your site. But geophys also seemed to show that one end of the range of buildings is just outside it, so Katie-Jane is sent off to talk to the foreman. Can she persuade him to let you box off an extra few metres of the building site to see if you can find the rest of your building? Yes, she can – in thirty seconds flat.

When you clean the rubble from round the walls, terracotta roof tiles turn up as well as lumps of mortar. But the finds you're most interested in are the fragments of plaster. Some of them are painted. There are dark reds, pinks and whites. Then you discover a little piece with tiny painted leaves on it. A few minutes later you uncover another bit with what looks like folds of a white costume all over it, and finally something that looks suspiciously like a bare leg. Walls painted as elaborately as this mean you've found the home of someone pretty opulent.

Small fragments of wall plaster from Turkdean, Gloucestershire. These pieces show the use of white, dark red, yellow and blue on the walls of this Roman villa.

Chedworth Roman villa, Gloucestershire.Hypocaust system showing red clay tile 'pilae' or columns holding up a mosaic floor, thus allowing the hot air to circulate beneath.

Next you look at the Roman wall your Anglo-Saxon warrior's grave was chopped through. It's part of a room that has got a lot of broken red, square, clay tiles scattered all over it, and underneath are a lot of similar tiles arranged in columns on the floor. Among the fragments there are also pieces of long, rectangular, red tile with wavy grooves on, and some of them have got bits of mortar stuck to them. All this is definite evidence that your Roman house had an underfloor heating system or 'hypocaust'. It helps to explain a dark, charcoaled area on the other side of the wall, which is probably all that's left of the stoke-hole where the fire that heated the system was originally situated. Hot air from that fire circulated round the pillars of red tiles supporting the floor of the room. It then rose up through flues also made of red tiles which were set in the walls. Your pieces of wavy-lined tiles are the remains of these upright heating flue-pipes. The wavy grooves were used to ensure that the mortar stuck to the tiles more easily.

Until now, every piece of archaeology you've discovered has been recorded and then dismantled to see what's underneath it. But Sinead decides that, as this area with the walls and hypocaust will soon be under the car-park, she'll simply cover it over and leave it intact for future generations who may be interested in it long after the car-park, and indeed the car, have become redundant.

Plan of the Roman Villa.
Note Katie-Jane's boxed-off
extension at the top.

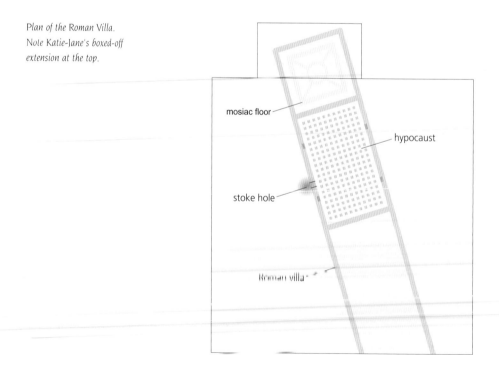

mosiac floor

hypocaust

stoke hole

Roman villa

Left and below: *Fragments of mosaic revealed in a garden excavation in Cirencester. At some time, the mosaic has been very badly repaired!*

When the evaluation was being done, one of the initial trenches showed two walls at right-angles, and in the angle between them were traces of mosaic. Carefully you clean inside the far corner of the range of buildings, hoping you might find a patch of mosaic floor.

Suddenly your trowel scrapes against something harder than the earth you've been cleaning. You trowel really gingerly now and come down on some little muddy squares. You recognize them as Roman tesserae. You dab at them with a wet sponge. As the mud's washed away you can see that some are white and others black. Gradually a chequerboard pattern emerges. You're nervous about working on such an exquisite piece of archaeology, but Sinead encourages you to carry on under her supervision. Roman floors were well made and are pretty robust. As long as you're particularly careful at the edges or in any patches that look worn, you should be fine. After fifteen minutes or so, you begin to uncover a second pattern called 'guilloche', which is made out of red

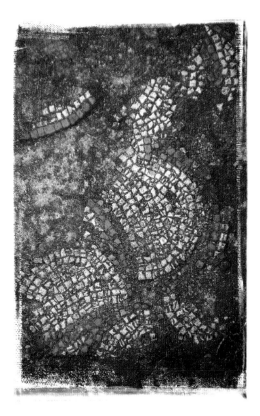

Fragments of mosaic being revealed at Cirencester.

and yellow tesserae and looks like little pieces of twisted rope. Is this the border of something really elaborate? You work inwards towards the centre of the room and come across even more patterns, and then pictures of small circular medallions. Then more pink and brown areas, until an hour and a half later a head begins to emerge.

Not all the mosaic is perfect. There's a large area that's clearly been mended by someone who wasn't all that bothered about the quality of their work. The tesserae are bigger and misshapen, some of them are made of broken roof tiles, while others are clearly the wrong colour. In some parts, including the face, there are bits missing where burrowing rodents have dislodged the little squares, or where later generations have driven their posts and stakes. Tree roots have also made their mark. Nevertheless Sinead's got a smile on her face. On average only one new Roman mosaic floor turns up each year in Britain.

Next day two mosaic recorders drive down from Durham to try to interpret the floor in detail. They look at it in silence for a long time, then there's a long whispered conversation, followed by a lot of looking things up in books. Finally they tell you that the mosaic was made by the Southern Central Group of mosaicists, most likely in the third century AD. These mosaicists were probably a group of families who lay low in the winter months making their tesserae and travelled hundreds of miles in the spring and summer laying beautiful floors in posh houses. The specialists say your mosaic is 'finely executed if rather simple work', which you think is a bit of a cheek. You'd have it on your floor any time. But they're back in your good books when they tell you they've identified the head. It's the demi-god 'Summer', so this room might well have been a summer dining room.

None of the archaeologists had expected such a fantastic find but next day, as the last shovelfuls of rubble are being cleared from around the mosaic, something even more tantalizing crops up. A green stain appears among the debris. It's carefully cleaned and soon it becomes apparent that it's a ring. But not just any old ring. There are some marks on it. Could they be someone's name? Could you have tangible evidence of a Roman who lived here 1,800 years ago? You'll have to wait until the conservator has worked her magic.

But what about the building that the owner of this ring lived in? For a start, how big was it? The archaeologists now know it stops in Katie-Jane's boxed-off extension. But it's extremely likely that it extends further south into your garden because of the evidence you've already found. Comparing it with similar ranges of buildings discovered in other places, it's likely that there are at least two rooms beyond the one you've already excavated, one of which we know, from the tesserae found in your garden, had another mosaic in it. So this may well have been a very big villa. But given that nothing else this size has been found within at least twenty square miles of here, maybe it's something more than that. Is it a major power centre? Could it possibly even be the provincial governor's palace?

There's a saying in archaeology: 'One stone's a stone, two are a wall, three are a building and four mean you've got a palace'. In other words, it's very easy to let your imagination run away with you. On the other hand, if archaeology is simply reduced to a series of dry-as-dust observations about post-holes, linear features and contexts, but gives no picture of human life in the past, then what's the point of it all? And, just as importantly, why should anyone bother to fund it?

Archaeologists have always attempted to interpret their work. It's a basic human need to create narratives that try to make sense of the world, and many archaeologists have become magnificent story-tellers. But the problem is that when we tell stories, they're coloured by who we are. Victorian antiquarians saw life through the prism of their public schools and the imperial world in which they lived, and this tended to be reflected in their archaeological interpretations. Today, if a Christian, a Zionist and a Palestinian archaeologist made exactly the same discovery on a site in Israel, they'd almost certainly come to entirely different conclusions about it. Modern British archaeologists tend to be interested in subjects like the breakdown of society, environmental impact and women's role in the community, so they look for evidence related to these issues on which they then base their conclusions about a site.

All of this is understandable, but it does mean that it's virtually impossible to be wholly objective when making interpretations. So on one hand interpretation is important, but on the other it can't be trusted.

Let's suppose for example that in fifty years' time there's a trade dispute about bananas between Costa Rica and Guatemala. This escalates into a full-blown nuclear war. A holocaust ensues. Human life struggles on for a few years but gradually becomes extinct. Another thousand years pass before archaeologists from the planet P'Tink land in your back garden and excavate the ruins of Tesbury's supermarket. What will they make of it?

FELLOW CITIZENS OF P'TAK

Our expedition embarked on a sub-surface survey which showed a complex structure at one end of the site. Ten evaluation trenches were dug covering 4 per cent of the area.

On the basis of this evaluation an area of six untargs was cleared of all overlying soil and green life-forms. An astonishingly vivid picture of an alien and yet strangely familiar culture was revealed. Extensive hard, flat, fabricated surfaces were discovered. These seem to be a distinguishing characteristic of this civilization. They were chequered with white linear markings on which were discovered beautifully painted icons such as 'ON WAY ON', 'ETROL' and 'ABLED PARKIN'. It can only be hoped that one day the significance of these icons will be understood. The sub-surface survey had revealed a significant metal concentration below this surface in one specific spot. Our laser-guided trowels made a remarkable find at this location when a magnificent hydrocarbon-fuelled metal transport container was uncovered there. It had clearly been deliberately buried, and at some time its upper surface had been attacked with metal implements. After considerable conservation work, a beautiful example of an internal wheel was revealed. On it the inscription 'FORD ANGL ' was still clearly visible in chrome inlay.

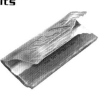

Tiny, exquisite, loose-leaved, perfectly-preserved book, found in a muddy deposit.

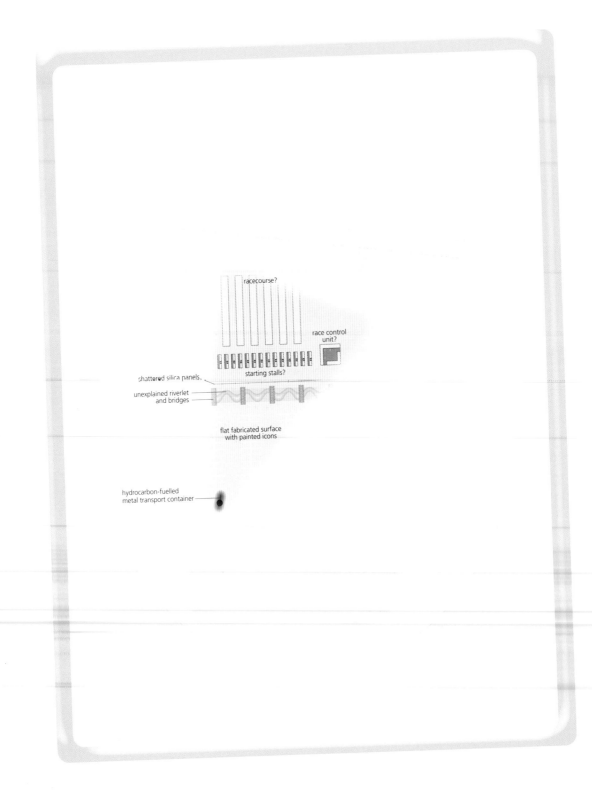

racecourse?

race control
unit?

shattered silica panels.

starting stalls?

unexplained riverlet
and bridges

flat fabricated surface
with painted icons

hydrocarbon-fuelled
metal transport container

At the north end of the chequered area was a barrier of shattered translucent silica panels. Over the top of this barrier and behind it, a tangled mass of metal sheets was evident. Given the amount of energy the fabrication of such metal would generate, this building must have been of very high status, and our first thoughts were that it could be the palace of a local governor. Strewn among the debris were collapsed concrete and brick turrets and battlements. Certainly this building either belonged to a life-form under threat, or one which wanted to announce its military might in order to impress the local inhabitants.

Also among the debris were the remnants of a considerable number of long, wide, metal tubes and what appear to have been several large metal boxes containing propellers. The stratification seems to imply that these were originally attached to the ceiling or roof area. Research is currently being undertaken into the challenging theory, particularly in view of the lightweight building materials, that this whole magnificent structure was not only a building but also a primitive form of flying vehicle similar to our early saucers.

When this context (Context 16) was removed, vast numbers of broken white tubes were discovered below it. Our conservation experts washed, cleaned and reassembled these beautiful objects. They were remarkably well made and artfully assembled, using very thin transparent silica. They reinforce the thesis that this whole complex represents the aesthetic pinnacle of this civilization.

Thin. silica 'Encouraging Tubes'.

Once this debris layer had been meticulously cleaned and six-dimensional recording had taken place, the extent of the building became apparent. A highly polished, artificial stone floor was revealed which even in its ruined state was seen to be finely executed if rather simple work. (It is now thought to have been made by the 'IKEA' school of polished floor-makers, probably an itinerant family who spent the cold part of the planet's rotation of its star polishing paving slabs, and the warmer part travelling hundreds of untargs laying beautiful floors for the local aristocracy.)

The bulk of this floor area was divided into seven parallel aisles which appear to have been separated by screens of metal and silica vertical embayments. Numerous icons were discovered which may originally have been attached to these screens. These included 'WO FOR THE PRIC OF ONE', 'ORRY TEMPO   OUT' and 'WINE OF THE WEE'.

At the end of each aisle, close to the shattered barrier, was a constricted access unit. These are very complex structures, but the most intact example, protected under a large heavy roofing sheet, seemed to preserve the main features. It consisted of what appeared to be a metal rotating mechanism next to which was a transparent horizontal silica plate. Behind the rotating mechanism were three batons bearing the icon 'NEXT CUSTOMER PLEA'. Behind the console was a four-legged revolving object clearly designed to swivel, and beyond the batons were the remnants of a rudimentary piece of computer equipment – a vivid picture of a time when technology had barely advanced beyond the cave-painting. There was a sliding compartmentalized tray below the computer. Was this designed for the storage of jewellery or tokens? Perhaps the beings who visited this primitive computer held it in such awe that regular offerings were made to it.

At one end of the row of consoles was the base of what appeared to be a much larger unit. Sherds from at least five different computers were found inside this base, along with the inscription 'STOMER SERVICE'. A smaller inscription below it is particularly fascinating. It reads 'ARTY PACKS OF ESBURYS COLA 3 EUROS'. This is the first discovered use of the icon 'COLA', one which has profoundly influenced our understanding of this life-form.

Apart from the wealth of building materials, the most numerous finds were aluminium tubular containers bearing this same icon 'COLA'. Aluminium is prohibitively costly to produce, yet these artefacts are notable not only for their ubiquity, but also for the beautiful manner in which they were crafted. These delightful objects would have been treasured by those who possessed them. It stretches credibility to believe they were wantonly discarded. Comparison with similar sites and artefacts from other galaxies leads us to the conclusion that they were deposited at sacred sites by a population fearful of outside attack, or as a response to some natural disaster. We await with interest scientific analysis of the residual deposits inside these containers, but preliminary research suggests the contents consists of a cocktail of powerful chemicals, possibly used to induce hallucinations during religious rites. So universal does the deposition of these tubes appear to be, that it is not unreasonable to define this life-form by that particular characteristic. Indeed, in his scholarly work of the same name, Professor Tritritrit P'Phoon has dubbed this species 'The Cola People', an appellation which seems particularly appropriate.

A number of four-wheeled chariots with latticed metal frames were also discovered. Of particular interest is the fact that none of these vehicles, despite considerable research, could be made to move in a straight line. There are also similar much smaller latticed frames, but these appear to have been without wheels. A radical, but doubtless erroneous, suggestion has been made that these could be shopping baskets. A much more plausible explanation is that they are ceremonial crash helmets worn by the chariot drivers. No mechanism has yet been discovered to power them, although the presence of ritual contact bars indicates that they may have been pushed, possibly by priests or slaves.

Associated with the large 'STOMER SERVICE' unit and within the same context as its five computers, equipment which our analysts believe to be a sound relay system was discovered. This would seem to imply that the extra-sensory perception of the Cola People was very limited.

Possible ceremnnial starting pistul.

Also in this context a finely-wrought ceremonial weapon was found.

So how can we explain this magnificent assemblage of artefacts and other phenomena? The initial suggestion that this is a governor's palace now seems to be untenable. There are no settlement areas, and the cooking and food processing areas would appear to indicate mass on-site catering rather than domestic use. Indeed, apart from a small broken object which has been interpreted as a tentacle cleaner there are few indications of the kind of ordinary everyday life we would expect to find in a residence. Thus we are thrown back onto our model of a ritual site. And while it would be absurd to draw final conclusions from such a small sample of this extensive civilization, some things are abundantly clear.

The 'Cola People' once used hydrocarbon-fuelled transport containers. But our excavation found only one example, and this was not in a context contemporary with the ritual complex. Rather, it was buried under, and is therefore earlier than, the white chequered hard surfaces. We conclude that this container was a dedicatory offering at an earlier phase of the site's development, and given that we have found no such containers in a later context, it seems reasonable to assume that by the time of the temple phase, these metal containers had become obsolete.

As to the ritual activities conducted in the complex, the wealth of finds has enabled us to develop a highly complex hypothesis, 'the Processual Racing Model'. In this model we see the initiates lined up in their chariots at the constricted access units, perhaps donating ritual tokens or 'NEXT CUSTOMER PLEA' batons. Once the ceremonial starting pistol had been fired, they set off down the aisles lined with enthusiastic and presumably cheering fellow members of this diminutive life-form who are seated on the vertical embayments, holding aloft their fluorescent 'encouraging tubes' which may well have contained various coloured liquids representing the different teams and competitors. Indeed, it may well be that icons such as 'Wine of the Wee ' delineated the areas for the various supporters in order to prevent outbreaks of violence. The course of the chariots down the aisles must have been erratic and dangerous. However, it is clear that some degree of order was maintained from the 'STOMER SERVICE' console overlooking the track. How different the noise and mayhem in the ritual building must have been from the contemplative quiet of the empty chequered area outside!

A number of our research students have attempted to explain a confused zone of small bridges, collapsed turrets and possible water features between the silica sheets and the hard surfaces, but whether viewed from a functional,

Inscribed Chitect brick.

spiritual or an aesthetic viewpoint no sense can yet be made of them. One possible clue may lie in a small inscription, 'CHITECT – ROD M', found carved on a broken piece of brick. It surely will not be long before our visual communication specialists are able to interpret this apparent dedication.

As to the punishments meted out to the losers and the rewards heaped on the winners of this ceremonial race, that is beyond the brief of our exploration. We should not simply assume that because the victor at our own weekly Interplanetary Noot'Hoo League is made Grand Harknit and the losers have their snims removed, something similar would necessarily apply here. But one final find, discovered on the very last day of our investigation, has a particularly haunting resonance: this exquisite ring engraved with the icon 'PULL', perhaps the name of the High Priest who once oversaw the ritual games at this fascinating site.

For their generous sponsorship of this project, grateful thanks to Interstellar Spacefuels PLC. We look forward to developing our relationship with this forward-looking company in the hope that we may discover more about the enigmatic Cola People, a life-form so far away and yet in many ways so like ourselves.

Sacred Cola ring.

Before the job of exploring Norton's Field is over, there's one mystery left to excavate: the dark moist area in the corner of the field near the portaloos. You check that this damp patch hasn't been caused by a recent leak and, once you're reassured, a team of three of you clean the whole area. It doesn't seem to your inexperienced eye to be particularly different from the rest of the site. There's the occasional piece of Roman pottery, and stray bits of worn medieval pot. The only thing you don't recall having seen elsewhere is a scattering of small sharp stones that you assume are natural.

In fact, they're not. They're flint, and there's no natural flint for miles around. This stone was brought here by human beings long ago. It's your first indication of prehistoric activity.

There are little pieces of flint like this lying about all over Britain. Why? Because flint-working has been the major tool-making technique used by human beings for the vast majority of the time we've existed on this planet. For over half a million years our ancestors were whacking away at lumps of flint in order to produce tools and implements.

Above: *A selection of long blades, detached from a core and ready to be further worked into implements.*
Opposite: *Flint knapping. Notice the use of a soft hammer made of deer antler and the waste flakes on the floor.*

Four thousand or so years ago a Bronze Age tool-maker would have sat in Norton's Field with a collection of flint nodules which would have come from the nearest source of chalk that contained flint. He or she would have chosen a suitable-looking nodule, then begun hitting it with a large pebble specially chosen for the purpose. They'd have knocked off the end of it to give themselves a flat platform to work off. Then they'd have started striking downwards, knocking off more pieces of flint to be made into tools. But in the process of shaping these tools they'd also have chipped off smaller, irregular flakes of flint rather like woodchips off a piece of timber to be used for construction. You've found some of these waste flakes.

Of course, techniques of flint-working had changed through time. Our earliest ancestors produced a single hand-axe from each nodule. These were often beautiful pieces of work but they not only wasted a lot of valuable raw material, they also gave you only one, rather cumbersome, tool. Later flint-knappers became much more sophisticated. They learnt how to make long, parallel-sided blades from each piece of flint. These were a much more efficient way of making cutting edges, could be mass-produced, were extremely adaptable and could be turned to a host of different uses. Some would have been fixed into a wooden shaft to make arrows and others were made into drills, knives or scrapers. A handful could be fitted into a piece of wood to create a sickle. By the Bronze Age, people had made an epoch-changing discovery. They'd learnt how to make shiny, new, flexible metal objects and in the process, many of the old specialized flint-knapping skills became redundant. Nevertheless a big lump of flint was still their Swiss army knife for day-to-day use.

In this new moist area you're exploring, at least twenty pieces of flint have now turned up. If you'd found only a few you might have concluded that in the Bronze Age this field was a brief stopping place where prehistoric people trimmed a few weapons during a journey. But there must be more to it than that. Maybe there was a settlement here.

You collect all the debris very carefully and each piece is surveyed in. A specialist should be able to tell, by putting some of the stone chippings back together again, how skilled the tool-makers were, and how they worked out which bit of their flint core to hit each time they wanted to make a new tool.

But the story of this part of the site is becoming more complicated. As you clean away from the flint scatter, you start to discover shards of grotty dark pottery: big rough pieces unlike any you've seen before. These aren't from the Bronze Age. They're the remnants of Iron Age pots and, given the size of the sherds, it looks as though there wasn't only Bronze Age activity around here but Iron Age as well. In one cleaning session you seem to have identified two more phases of activity and taken the age of your site back another 2,000 years!

Iron Age pottery sherds. Note the rim at the top of each piece.

The history of tools

We've already discussed the Stone Age, the Bronze Age and the Iron Age, but in fact the vast majority of things made in all these ages were constructed from wood and other organic materials that haven't survived. So we get a very distorted view of what people actually possessed in the past.

For instance, take the history of tools. Archaeologists have found a variety of stone scrapers, blades, knives, axes and arrowheads from the Stone and Bronze Ages. By the Iron Age all these stone tools had been replaced by metal ones. But once the Romans left Britain, we don't see many changes in tool technology until the 1920s, when suddenly tools were being made from newly invented materials like plastic. Then from the 1950s onwards came the Power Tool Age with the advent of the Black and Decker drill and the Bosch circular saw.

This tends to be the way that prehistoric information is often presented. It's easy to imagine it on a big poster pinned up in a secondary school classroom. But it's an extremely partial view of human history!

A flint core. At the top is the striking platform; down the sides can be seen the facets where blades have been detached.

When you've finished cleaning, you're not sure whether you've come down on to natural geology or if you've got some sort of deposit created by human beings. There's only one way to resolve it. You have to get down on your hands and knees and start cleaning all over again. This is pretty frustrating. You've already cleaned the surface once. But after a while the other two diggers say they think they can make out a slightly darker curving line about a metre wide in one corner of the area. At first you think they're hallucinating, but then you begin to suspect that you can see it too. Then, as the cleaning progresses, the curve comes clearly into focus. It must be man-made. What should you do with it?

By now of course you know the answer. Put a section in it to find out what's there and how deep it is.

It turns out to be about half a metre in depth with a few more flint flakes at the bottom. In the side of the section is a large curving piece of pot. It's buff coloured, with a rough surface and lots of lumps in the clay. As you clear the section back and the earth away, you reveal more and more of it. You can see its shape now and none of it's broken. Does this mean you've got a complete, intact pot in your trench, possibly thousands of years old? You record the situation as it is, then to find out more you extend the section.

The Bronze Age burial urn.

Inverted Bronze Age cremation urn excavated at Winterbourne Gunner.

The urn is bound up in bandages ready for lifting and taking to the conservation laboratory (see page 97).

Almost immediately, up near the surface, you come across the bottom of the pot. In other words the whole thing's upside-down. You carry on down until it's completely exposed. It's perfect! Not a break in it! But what is it? It looks like a small version of an Ali Baba pot, in which a very tiny thief could have hidden. It's only 50 centimetres high and has a rolled, rounded rim. Its base is narrow and it widens out towards the rim. All over the top third of the pot are markings in the clay that were made by stabbing something into it to make a regular pattern. It's a Bronze Age burial urn, about three and a half thousand years old.

The cremated bone from the Winterbourne Gunner urn – unusually there are large pieces of well-preserved bone, which are from a well-built, mature male.

Inside it there should be a mass of cremated human bone. It'll need a lot of work to sort it out. The conservator is on site working on the medieval knife-blade, so you call her over. She produces a great roll of bandage from the back of her battered Citroën van. Over a matter of hours she slowly and lovingly wraps it round the pot, then lifts the whole thing into a cardboard box packed with bubble wrap. Soon it's disappeared into her van and off to the museum.

There wasn't much information from either geophys or from the evaluation trenches about this end of the site. But the presence of this urn seems to show that there was plenty of prehistoric activity here. Not only that, but it's pretty significant activity. The metre-wide line is almost certainly all that's left of a 'ring' ditch. There would once have been a Bronze Age burial mound here, which would have looked like a giant, upturned breakfast bowl with a ditch round it. And if there's one cremation urn in this kind of ditch, there are usually more.

They're often arranged as several burials round a central one. In order to find out if this is the case here, you empty out the rest of the ditch material, but disappointingly you don't discover anything new.

There are other places to look though. What about the area inside the curve of your ditch, the place where there might originally have been the mound? You'll explore it tomorrow.

That night is a late one. Tomorrow will be the final day of the entire dig, and Sinead has put a hundred pounds behind the bar of the local pub so the diggers can have a farewell party. A few of them have got work to go to on other excavations, but the rest will be unemployed. All of them find it virtually impossible to live on a digger's wages. Two of them think they'll go back to university to get more qualifications to improve their job prospects. Two more are giving up archaeology altogether even though they love it. They're going to try to get jobs in computer programming instead. Another's going into telephone sales.

Next morning Frankie turns up on her bike to pay one of her periodic visits to monitor progress on the site. After discussion, she and Sinead agree that the rest of the barrow area should be excavated.

You're asked to help excavate the part where the Bronze Age mound would have been. You work there for some time, but it seems fruitless. Should you stop now? There's lots of recording and tidying away still to be done, and only a few hours left to do it. Then you get a glimpse of something greyish white that might be a stone. Or might not. It's human bone. As you peel the earth away you uncover a very ancient skeleton. But it's remarkably small. In fact it's so small it's probably a child, and it's buried in a very odd position.

The more you dig, the clearer the picture becomes. Frankie can tell by looking at the teeth that the body is that of a seven- or eight-year-old, and it's crouched in a foetal position in a shallow pit, in what would have been the edge of the mound. There's also a solitary find close by. It's a flint arrow-head with a barb on either side to hold it firmly in its victim. It's not lodged in a bone, but you think you can see a couple of nicks in the ribs. Could the arrow have pierced the child's flesh and caused a fatal wound? Two of the diggers lift the little child's skeleton, and you work on. The way the ditch curves seems to imply that you've got what was once the centre of the mound in your area. Despite a couple of cleanings, you can't see a trace of any central burial. It may be there isn't one here, or perhaps it just isn't showing up at

An impression of how the Bronze Age child might have looked when originally buried might distress some people today, but for most of human history, people have had a very different attitude towards death. See page 118.

this level. Maybe it's been completely ploughed away. In fact there's very little of interest here apart from a few burnt grains in a shallow pit. Are they worth keeping? Probably not, but you bag them up anyway. It's decided to dig a sondage to see if there's anything below. This will have the added benefit of sorting out whether the dark subsoil on each side of the barrow ditch is natural geology or re-deposited material.

You peg out a 1 x 1 metre test-pit and dig down half a metre. There's no more archaeology here. The archaeologists are now absolutely convinced that this is natural material. There's no point digging down any further – instead, they want to extend the trench to find out more about the barrow. If they don't do it today, they never will. But it's already nearly 12.30 p.m., and work's almost at a standstill because it's teeming with rain. As you trudge back to the portacabin for an early

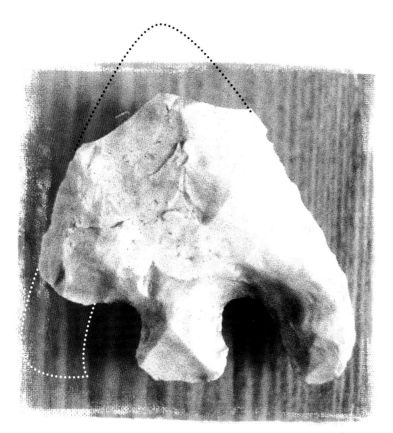

Bronze Age barbed and tanged arrowhead, with the point and one of the tangs missing.

lunch you have to accept the harsh reality that you've run out of time. Soon all your work will be covered up again, and the builders will move across to your end of the site. You'll record the barrow, then let it all stay put for the next hundred years or so, protected by the asphalt of the new Tesbury's car-park.

You stare out at the rain. It occurs to you that it's an amazing coincidence that there should have been two ancient human burials on your site. Sinead agrees you've been lucky, but explains that most early prehistoric archaeology is to do with burials, and the big monuments associated with them. There are Neolithic long barrows and henge monuments, round barrows, stone circles and standing stones from the Bronze Age – in fact all the paraphernalia that so fascinated antiquarians such as John Aubrey and William Stukeley. These great, mysterious structures were places people used when they were worshipping, celebrating and burying their dead. It's only in the later prehistoric period that we find hill forts, field systems, settlements and other smaller finds that we associate with everyday life.

EARLY PREHISTORIC SITES

These great mysterious structures were places
people used when they were worshipping,
celebrating and burying their dead.

*Right: Inside the burial chamber at Stoney
Littleton in Somerset, showing the passage
and the side chambers for burials.*

Above: *Air photograph
of Winterbourne Stoke barrow
group, showing, on the left,
an earthen long barrow,
looking like a linear
bank, and a great variety
of different-shaped
round barrows.*

*Air view of Avebury in
Wiltshire, showing the
earthworks of this henge
monument – a massive bank
outside a deep ditch.*

The neolithic long barrow at Stoney Littleton, Somerset.

Harold's Stones. A stone row at Trelleck in Monmouthshire.

Below: *A stone circle at Gors Fawr in Pembrokeshire.*

LATER PREHISTORIC SITES

It's only later on that we find hill forts, field systems and settlements which we associate with everyday life.

Air view of Barbury Castle, in Wiltshire, near Swindon, with multiple ramparts and ditches.

Right: *Prehistoric and Roman fields on Fifield Down, Wiltshire. These slight banks show us where arable fields were in Prehistoric times.*

Below: *Butser in Hampshire. A reconstruction of what an Iron Age farm may have looked like.*

The reconstructed Iron Age house at Butser in Hampshire.

The rain's almost stopped. You go outside and start bailing out your trench with a hard hat. You'd forgotten to take in a pile of context sheets. They're soaked and you'll have to write them out again. You're hungover, depressed and, although the whole barrow has now been excavated, no more finds or burials have turned up.

Then there's a shout from just outside the Roman building. The newly wet ground is showing up a black circular stain that wasn't visible when the earth was dry. It's a pit. Two of the diggers put a section through it, and at half past four, just an hour before your final goodbyes, they come up with the very last finds from the site. They triumphantly show you five clay moulds for making bronze axe-heads. At last here's proof positive that people were working here at least three and a half thousand years ago making sophisticated Bronze Age weapons.

Then it's 5.30 p.m. The diggers, the portacabins and the portaloos trundle off site. You think it's all over. But in fact it's hardly begun!

Digging is only the tip of the archaeological iceberg. The site's empty, the builders have moved in, work's begun on Rod's wondrous neo-Venetian erection, but more archaeologists are working on the archaeological finds than ever before.

The first and most important job is to make sure you've made a coherent and accurate record of the site. The archaeology lay in the ground for hundreds and even thousands of years before being dismantled and carted off into storage. You may think you understand it but, unless the record is complete, future archaeologists won't be able to work out what you did, and all your labour and the destruction of the site will have been for nothing. So the mounds of papers have to be put in order. The context sheets, the site plans and the notebooks must be correlated and cross-referenced, the photos and slides labelled, and the finds processed and distributed to the various specialists who've agreed to write reports on them. Other bits and pieces, like the environmental evidence and samples from the various pits and ditches, have to be sent off too for processing and study.

Sinead produces an assessment report after her initial examination of the finds to see what further level of detailed work is needed. This report is very important. In days gone by a huge amount of archaeology either went unrecorded or the records and finds were lost. Nowadays it's the duty of the archaeologist in charge to make sure there's an accessible report which interested parties can refer to. Tesbury's get a copy (which is fair enough considering they're paying for it), as do the Site and Monuments Record and the National Monuments Record in Swindon. And you're particularly pleased that, as the person who initially discovered the site, you get your own copy together with a fulsome acknowledgement of the work you did in your garden and at Norton's Field.

A final report will be written, courtesy of Tesbury's, when all the information about the site is finally in, so it'll be some time before Sinead gets down to this. Mind you, she'll have to adhere to pretty strict deadlines. Westhampton Archaeology Trust needs to make money, and will want her freed up to start work on another job as soon as possible.

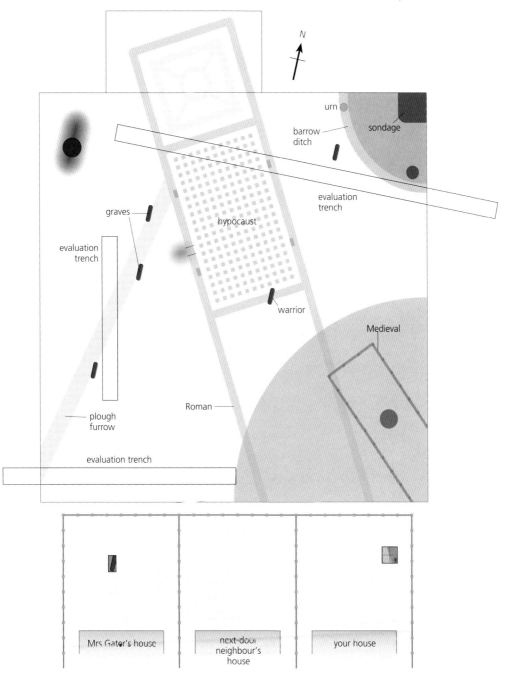

The plan of features in the open area excavation.

N

urn

sondage

barrow ditch

evaluation trench

graves

hypocaust

evaluation trench

warrior

Medieval

plough furrow

Roman

evaluation trench

Mrs Gater's house

next-door neighbour's house

your house

Gradually, new discoveries are made. Some simply confirm what the field-archaeologists had already deduced, but others are a surprise. The pottery analysts say there's much more Iron Age pot on the site than anyone had appreciated. Likewise, the Bronze Age specialists have identified many more flint flakes and a few extra flint implements which, because they're stratified, show beyond doubt that people settled somewhere round here in the Bronze and Iron Ages.

You'd forgotten that Shahid, the student from the local university, had taken a lot of heavy metal samples, and his analysis provides an unexpected additional clue. He says that in the south-west of the site where most of the prehistoric activity seems to be, there's a big build-up of lead and zinc traces which could be evidence of settlement. If Iron or Bronze Age people lived in Norton's Field, it was probably somewhere near your back garden.

The prehistoric experts have done some radiocarbon dating. The cremated bone in the urn gives a date around 1600 BC, and the little skeleton is from about 2000 BC. The bone specialists have discovered something astonishing – the child was severely disabled. Its auditory meati (the ear-holes in its skull) are virtually non-existent. This means he or she would have been chronically deaf and probably wouldn't have been able to speak either. It's a sad story, but it also shows that despite these problems, the little mite was sufficiently well cared for during its brief life to survive the rigours of the early Bronze Age, and even when it died the child was treated with respect. But how did it die? Was it shot by an enemy, or by one of the community? Could it have been involved in a tragic accident, or was the arrow-head nothing to do with its death? Maybe it was just a victim of infant mortality. Another riddle you won't be able to solve.

Other radiocarbon tests show your barrow was built around 2100 BC. So it was shortly after its construction that the little child was buried in the side of it. Five hundred years later it was still a recognized burial site, sufficiently revered for a cremated burial to be dug into the now silted-up ditch that ran round it.

The osteo archaeologists have been looking at the bones from your cemetery. Very unusually, all of the Anglo-Saxons had broken at least one limb or rib during their lives, and one poor soul had osteoporosis. Two of the women had osteoarthritis even though they were relatively young, and three of them show signs of having suffered as children. X-rays of their long bones had shown marks called Harris Lines, which show that their growth had been temporarily interrupted when they were young – this implies that at some time they'd either lived on a very poor diet or had gone through some terrible experience. Clearly, living in Norton's Field in the Dark Ages was tough going.

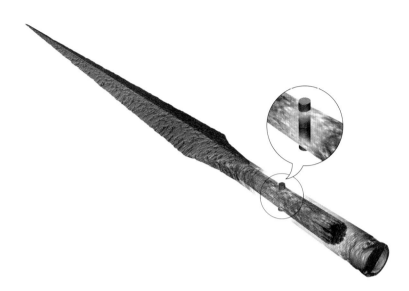

*Anglo-Saxon spearhead with
the detail of the rivet which
held the spearhead onto the
shaft, part of which remains.*

The DNA tests have come back and, sure enough, five of your skeletons were related. Your cemetery seems to be a small one belonging to just one family.

There's exciting additional information from the conservation lab. The X-ray of the spearhead you found in the warrior's grave in Norton's Field shows that it has a hollow metal socket which was originally attached to a wooden shaft, and the remains of the rivet that held it in place are still visible. There's even a piece of the original wood inside the socket, and it's been identified as ash.

But possibly the most exciting work the conservator has been able to do is on the sword. There's no trace of the handle, which would have been made of wood or bone, and the pommel that protected the back of the fighter's hand is also missing. But the blade, over a metre long and pattern-welded, is virtually intact. And on it, picked out in niello, is a runic inscription. It's the name of the sword: 'Skull Splitter' – a title that has rung through the ages.

And what about the gash in the warrior's skull? It can't have been done by the mechanical digger because if it had, the cut would have been irregular and a different colour from the rest of the bone. This cut is smooth and the same colour as the bone round it. It was made by a sharp blade, almost certainly a large sword, and you're told the wound was fatal. You're initially sceptical that anyone could prove this. But apparently the experts say that, when the cut was

THE STORY OF NORTON'S FIELD

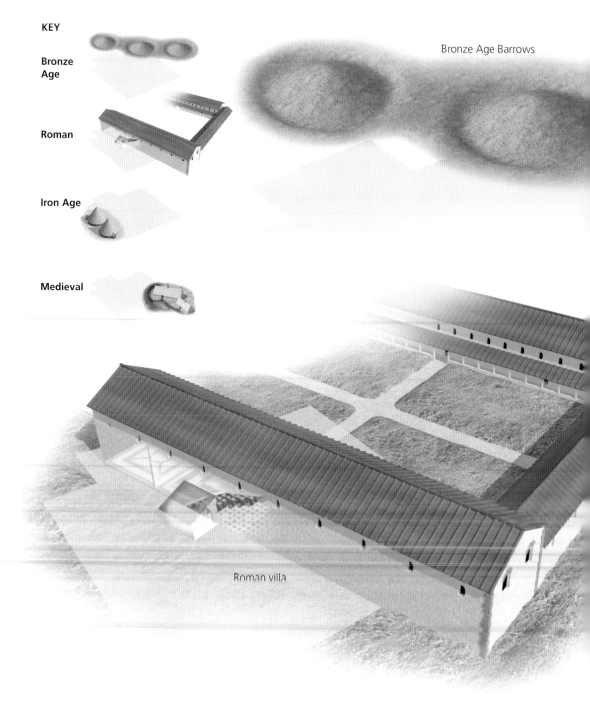

KEY

Bronze Age

Roman

Iron Age

Medieval

Bronze Age Barrows

Roman villa

A series of reconstructions showing where the barrows and buildings were originally located in the field. The pink is the area of the main excavation (see page 199).

Iron Age settlement

Medieval settlement

looked at under a scanning electron microscope, there was no evidence that any new bone had started to form round the edges of the cut. In other words, the warrior   if that's what he was   died shortly after the blow on his head.

There's one final piece of graphic evidence about his life and death. The environmentalist has examined the sample of soil taken from his stomach area. Shortly before he died, he had eaten an eel.

The niello on the knife found with the skeleton in Mrs Gater's garden has also been thoroughly cleaned and examined. The pattern is like the body of two intertwining snakes, and you particularly like the animal head at one end of it. It's a little dragon or some other weird creature.

The black earth from the Anglo-Saxon layers has been thoroughly scrutinized. This kind of deposit is very common in contexts from this period, particularly when they overlie Roman towns. The samples you found are made up of a lot of rotted vegetable matter, but the specialists aren't sure whether this is food remains from a settlement, or soil from a garden that had been manured with kitchen waste. The same problem exists on Anglo-Saxon sites all over the country. Once it's been solved, we'll understand much more about the settlement patterns of the mysterious people who inhabited our country after Roman government broke down. But a lot more work needs to be done before we'll get the answers we need.

The Roman pit under the wall has got a strange mixture of wood shavings and chippings in it, so once it may have been a place where the waste was dumped after timbers had been prepared for building. There are also lots of parasite eggs from the human gut here. Most people suffered from these parasites in the past, so the pit was probably a cesspit too – an early loo later filled with wood waste.

Sinead's Roman specialist is able to tell by looking at the pottery that there were Romans in Norton's Field from at least AD 150 to well beyond 300. The Samian ware from your garden doesn't appear in Britain until around AD 150, and disappeared around 250. But there are also colour-coated wares from Oxford and the New Forest which replaced Samian and didn't disappear until the Romans left Britain.

There's also the black-burnished ware which is common all over Britain, and lots of pieces of locally made grey and red wares. The specialists say the whole assemblage is typical of a long-lived rural settlement with a local villa. So bang goes your theory about the governor's palace!

Now the specialists have pulled all the evidence together, they're able to tell you that in pre-Roman times your street and Norton's Field were predominantly wooded, but by the time the Romans had arrived it had become open, cultivated countryside. Then, when they left, the trees sprang up again along with lots of weeds, until in medieval times the area began to be farmed again. Oddly, and most interestingly, the evidence from the prehistoric barrow ditch seems to show that the barrow wasn't built in open countryside but in a forest. What a strange sight it must have been half-hidden among trees! The likely construction date for the barrow has been established by carbon-dating the burnt grains you found in the shallow pit on the final day of the dig. It was built around 2100 BC plus or minus sixty years. You get a pat on the back for having found that grain. You don't mention that you nearly chucked it on the spoil-heap.

Sinead has come to one big conclusion. The geophys and the trenches show that the archaeology seems to taper out on the north side of the field. So if there was a major settlement around here in the Iron Age, not to mention in Roman and Saxon times and during the medieval period, she believes it's likely to have been under the houses where you and your neighbours now live. When she tells you this, you remember that barrows like the one you found evidence of aren't usually built on their own. There are almost certainly more around – possibly under your house! It seems as though you, Mrs Gater, and your next-door neighbour (who's now been sent to a safari park near Bognor Regis to be trained in leadership and survival skills) are simply the latest inhabitants of a settlement that's been in existence for the best part of 5,000 years. It's a sobering thought, but it also means that if your houses are ever knocked down, there's likely to be an archaeological goldmine underneath them. So Frankie has made sure that from now on they'll be recorded in the Sites and Monuments Record as an area of potential archaeological interest.

There's one question that's been nagging you. Who gets the finds? You learn that legally the ones that came out of the gardens belong to you and Mrs Gater, and everything in Norton's Field becomes the property of Tesbury's. But before they started work, the archaeology unit obtained an agreement that Tesbury's would hand over their finds to the County Museum. They do so, and you and Mrs Gater do the same.

Part of you feels like holding on to a few bits and pieces. After all you're probably more interested in them than anyone else; you certainly care about them more then anyone else! But there's no guarantee that when you die your relatives will feel the same. Every day small private collections of finds end up in a skip because the people who inherit them can't be bothered with them.

But you get your reward for being generous. Six months later you're invited to visit the local museum. It's the preview of an exhibition sponsored by Tesbury's PLC entitled 'From Stone Age to Supermarket – A History of Norton's Field'. As you sip your Tesbury's Chardonnay and nibble your Tesbury's mini-pizzas your heart swells with pride. You move from exhibit to exhibit watching the story of your field unfold, illustrated by the finds you dug, washed, labelled and recorded.

But you're even prouder when you attend the grand opening of the new supermarket. The museum has provided a small glass case of your finds which are on display in the entrance near the place where customers collect their shopping trolleys. More people will look at this in a month than ever visit the local museum.

And Tesbury's have made their own archaeological contribution. In pride of place, between the fish counter and the cooked meats, is a full-scale reproduction of your mosaic, with the demi-god Summer in all her glory smiling down on the halibut and plaice fillets.

The story isn't quite over. One evening Sinead phones you in a great excitement. The ring you found on almost the last day of the excavation has a name on the inside of it – Lucresia. But even more significant is the symbol on it. It's a Chi-Rho. This is the letter P with a multiplication sign at the bottom of it. The 'X' is the Greek letter CHI, and the P represents the letter RHO. These are the first two letters of the Greek word CHRISTOS, meaning Christ. They show that Lucresia was a Christian in Late-Roman Britain. It's a phenomenally rare find!

And that's about it. Out of the rubble, refuse and lost property of nearly 5,000 years of human activity, you were able to piece together the unfolding story of life and death in the area round your home. Was it worth all the hours of labour, the boring, repetitive scraping and cleaning back, the tedious recording, the bleeding knuckles, the cold, the damp and the aching limbs? Think about it. Archaeology is rubbish, isn't it?

Norton's Field is an archaeological dig to die for. In real life you'll seldom find the remnants of so many periods of British history so clearly delineated on one archaeological site. Most archaeologists have never found a Chi-Rho ring or an Anglo-Saxon sword, and Roman mosaic floors with human figures on them are very rare in Britain. But we wanted to give our readers as broad a picture of British archaeology as we could, so forgive us if, when you go on your first proper dig, it doesn't offer you quite the archaeological riches you discovered on your first virtual dig. We also apologize for not having dealt with Viking or Pictish archaeology. We've recommended a few books on these fascinating periods at the end of the book. Nevertheless, despite these caveats, if you dig for long enough you're bound to discover things that are just as exciting as the ones we've written about.

So if we've got you all fired up, what should you do next? How can you get involved in archaeology?

Most counties have their own archaeological society. These societies often run a museum, publish an annual journal (sometimes called 'proceedings') and many are engaged in field work or excavation projects. Most have a series of lectures through the winter months. There are also a host of smaller and more local societies. Your library, county museum or county archaeologist will usually know about these, how active they are and whether they're involved with a field project at present.

Another route into archaeology is to join the Council for British Archaeology, the national co-ordinating body based in York. Not only will they know of all the local groups and societies, they publish a magazine, *British Archaeology*, six times a year, and they also periodically issue lists of excavations with addresses to enable you to contact the right people with a view to getting involved. The CBA is divided into local regions, and membership of the national group entitles you to membership of your local regional group. Many of these groups publish their own newsletter, which has details of their local activities including lectures, day courses and so on. The newsletters also provide details of all the work that's going on in the region.

Another accessible magazine is *Current Archaeology*, which is published six times a year. It's very readable, informative and well illustrated, and there's an annual supplement called *The Archaeology Handbook* which lists excavations and organizations on a regional basis.

Most archaeologists find they need both these publications to keep up with what's happening. Both have links on the internet.

There's also the thriving Young Archaeologists' Club for younger enthusiasts, and the Time Team Club for addicts of the television series.

If you have more than a passing interest, you might like to think about taking a course to learn more through your local university, WEA or Adult Education Centre. Some universities still have a commitment to extra-mural teaching and traditionally archaeology has been one of the most popular subjects. There are nothing like the hundreds of courses that were put on in the 1960s and 1970s but there are still plenty of opportunities. Many universities offer a two-year 'Introduction to Archaeology' Certificate Course where you can learn about different aspects of the subject (often under the direction of very enthusiastic tutors), get involved in fieldwork and research and, if you want to, take a part-time degree.

So if you fancy reading more on the subject, what should you look at? There are, of course, lots of good books about. But beware! Some of them are really quite nutty. These usually involve ficticious ley lines, extraterrestrial

visits and lost civilizations, or provide definite proof that Atlantis is half a mile off the coast of Scarborough. Others are really only picture books – fine if you want nice views, but short on information. What we've done here is to try to point out the best, depending on the depth of your interest and how far you want to go.

For a broad picture of the whole subject the best book is Kevin Greene, *Archaeology, An Introduction* (now in its 4th edition – Routledge 2002). Also useful is Clive Gamble, *Archaeology: The Basics* (Routledge 2001).

There's also the dense (but useful for browsing and looking up items) tome by Colin Renfrew and Paul Bahn, *Archaeology: Theory, Methods and Practice* (Thames and Hudson, 3rd edition 2000). Anything written by Paul Bahn is well worth looking at.

The classic book on excavation is Philip Barker's *Techniques of Archaeological Excavation* (Batsford, first published in 1977 but with later editions). He followed this with *Understanding Archaeological Excavation* (Batsford 1986). A more recent and extremely useful book with the current methodology is John Collis, *Digging Up the Past: An Introduction to Archaeological Excavation* (Sutton 2001), which gives a very good idea of what it's like to work on an excavation.

On the world scale, an impression can be gained from *The Atlas of Archaeology* by Mick Aston and Tim Taylor (Dorling Kindersley 1998), or more comprehensively *Past Worlds: The Times Atlas of Archaeology* – Chris Scarre, general editor, with a galaxy of contributors (Times Books, 1995).

Specifically for Britain, there's the rather academic *Archaeology of Britain: An Introduction from the Upper Palaeolithic to the Industrial Revolution* edited by John Hunter and Ian Ralston (Routledge 1999). This largely replaces *Archaeology in Britain since 1945* edited by Ian Longworth and John Cherry (British Museum 1986), though the latter is still useful.

The most accessible book on geophysics is Anthony Clark, *Seeing Beneath the Soil: Prospecting Methods in Archaeology* (Batsford 1990). Burials and what we can learn from them are covered in Julian Richards, *Meet the Ancestors* (BBC 1999), *Making Faces* by John Prag and Richard Neave (British Museum 1997), Michael Parker Pearson, *The Archaeology of Death and Burial* (Sutton 1999), and *Earthly Remains: The History and Science of Preserved Human Bodies* by Andrew Chamberlain and Michael Parker Pearson (British Museum Press 2001), while forensic aspects are discussed in John Hunter, Charlotte Roberts and Anthony Martin, *Studies in Crime: An Introduction to Forensic Archaeology* (Batsford 1996).

For environmental archaeology, see Ian Simmons, *Environmental History: A Concise Introduction* (Blackwell 1993), and Petra Dark, *The Environment of Britain in the First Millenium AD* (Duckworth 2000). Also of great interest still is

John Evans, *The Environment of Early Man in the British Isles* (Paul Elek 1975). Dendrochronology is well explained in Mike Baillie's *A Slice through Time* (Batsford 1995), and the implications of such precise dating in his *Exodus to Arthur* (Batsford 1999).

For the prehistoric period the best introduction is Tim Darvill's *Prehistoric Britain* (Batsford 1987). Individual periods are covered in Nicholas Barton, *Stone Age Britain* (Batsford/English Heritage 1997), Michael Parker Pearson, *Bronze Age Britain* (Batsford/English Heritage 1993), which covers the Neolithic (or New Stone Age) period as well, and Barry Cunliffe, *Iron Age Britain* (Batsford/English Heritage 1995). See also Francis Pryor's book, *Seahenge: New Discoveries in Prehistoric Britain* (HarperCollins 2001).

For burial in this period and on into the Roman period, see *Dying for the Gods: Human Sacrifice in Iron Age and Roman Europe* by Miranda Aldhouse Green (Tempus 2001). Very relevant to the theme in this book is Ann Woodward, *British Barrows: A Matter of Life and Death* (Tempus 2000). For later burials, see *The Anglo-Saxon Way of Death: Burial Rites in Early England* by Sam Lucy (Sutton 2000).

For Wales, see Frances Lynch, Jeffrey Davies and Stephen Aldhouse Green, *Prehistoric Wales* (Sutton 2000). For Scotland, see Caroline Wickham-Jones, *Scotland's First Settlers* (1994), P. J. Ashmore, *Neolithic and Bronze Age Scotland* (1996), and Ian Armit, *Celtic Scotland* (1997) (all Batsford/Heritage Scotland volumes).

The Roman period in Britain is well covered. See especially Martin Millett, *Roman Britain* (Batsford/English Heritage 1995), and Guy de la Bédoyère, *The Golden Age of Roman Britain* (Tempus 1999). For Scotland, see David Breeze, *Roman Scotland* (Batsford/Historic Scotland 1996).

Of particular relevance to this book is Guy de la Bédoyère, *The Buildings of Roman Britain* (Tempus 2001).

The medieval period is now generally divided into early (pre-1066) and later (post-1066). General surveys of these periods include Martin Welch, *Anglo-Saxon England* (Batsford/English Heritage 1992), *The Anglo-Saxons* edited by James Campbell (Phaidon 1982), Julian D. Richards, *Viking Age England* (Batsford/English Heritage 1991), and Trevor Rowley, *Norman England* (Batsford/English Heritage 1997). A good general book is Colin Platt, *Medieval England: A Social History and Archaeology from the Conquest to 1600 AD* (Routledge 1978 and later editions). See also, though some are a little out of date, *The Archaeology of Anglo-Saxon England* edited by David Wilson (Cambridge 1976), John Steane, *The Archaeology of Medieval England and Wales* (Guild 1984), and Helen Clarke, *The Archaeology of Medieval England* (Colonnade 1984).

For the western and northern areas of Britain, where things can be very different, see Charles Thomas, *Celtic Britain* (Thames & Hudson 1997).

Since Wales and Scotland are not specifically covered in this book, it would be worth looking at Christopher Arnold and Jeffrey Davies, *Roman and Early Medieval Wales* (Sutton 2000), Mark Redknap, *The Christian Celts: Treasures of Late Celtic Wales* (National Museum of Wales 1991), and Mark Redknap, *Vikings in Wales: An Archaeological Quest* (National Museum of Wales 2000); and Sally Foster, *Picts, Gaels and Scots: Early Historic Scotland* (Batsford/Historic Scotland 1996), Anna Ritchie, *Viking Scotland* (Batsford/Historic Scotland 1993), and Peter Yeoman, *Medieval Scotland* (Batsford/Historic Scotland 1995).

For the post-medieval, historic or industrial periods, roughly from 1600, see David Crossley, *Post-Medieval Archaeology in Britain* (Leicester 1990), Richard Newman with David Cranstone and Christine Howard-Davies, *The Historical Archaeology of Britain c. 1540–1900* (Sutton 2001), and Michael Stratton and Barrie Trinder, *Industrial England* (Batsford/English Heritage 1997).

A particularly good survey is *The Age of Transition: The Archaeology of English Culture 1400–1600* edited by David Gaimster and Paul Stamper (Oxbow 1997).

For the integration of documentary, archaeological and burial information at the end of this period, see Margaret Cox, *Life and Death in Spitalfields 1700 to 1850* (Council for British Archaeology 1996).

Finally, there is a huge range of small booklets published by Shire Publications Ltd (Cromwell House, Church Street, Princes Risborough, Buckinghamshire HP27 9AA), which are superb inexpensive introductions to all sorts of aspects of archaeology.

Many sites, open to the public, have very good guide books – those of Cadw Welsh Historic Monuments are particularly useful and beautifully produced.

Tony Robinson presents Channel 4's archaeology series *Time Team*, and played Baldrick in *Blackadder*. He also devised and wrote four series of the BBC's *Maid Marian and Her Merry Men*, in which he played the Sheriff of Nottingham.

His awards as a writer of children's television programmes include two Royal Television Society awards, a BAFTA and the International Prix Jeunesse. He wrote thirty episodes of Central TV's *Fat Tulip's Garden*, a thirteen-part BBC series based on Homer's *Iliad* and *Odyssey* called *Odysseus – the Greatest Hero of Them All*, and twenty-six episodes of his Old Testament series *Blood and Honey*. He has also written seventeen children's books, including most recently *Tony Robinson's Book of Kings and Queens*.

He left school with four O-levels but has recently been awarded two honorary degrees; an MA for services to drama and archaeology from Bristol University in 1999, and one from the University of East London in 2002.

Mick Aston was born and brought up in the Black Country, the only son of a cabinet-maker. Following higher education at Birmingham University he has had a variety of archaeological jobs, including field officer at Oxfordshire County Museum, Woodstock, the first county archaeologist for Somerset, and academic posts at Oxford and Bristol. He is now Professor of Landscape Archaeology at the University of Bristol.

Since 1990 he has been involved in making television programmes for Channel 4 about archaeology, furthering his belief in popularizing archaeology and making it available to a much wider audience. He is best known for his role as co-presenter and archaeological consultant to Channel 4's highly popular *Time Team* programme, watched regularly by over three million viewers.

He has written, edited and co-authored eighteen books, including the best-selling *Mick's Archaeology*, and is happiest working with his postgraduate students.

Mick lives in North Somerset with his children, James and Katherine. In his rare spare time, he enjoys gardening, walking, classical music, cooking and travelling in his VW camper van.